MONITOR

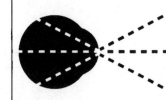

This Large Print Book carries the
Seal of Approval of N.A.V.H.

MONITOR

THE STORY OF THE LEGENDARY CIVIL WAR IRONCLAD AND THE MAN WHOSE INVENTION CHANGED THE COURSE OF HISTORY

James Tertius deKay

G.K. Hall & Co.
Thorndike, Maine

Copyright © 1997 by James Tertius deKay

Published in 1998 by arrangement with Walker Publishing
Company, Inc.

G.K. Hall Large Print Nonfiction Series.

The text of this Large Print edition is unabridged.
Other aspects of the book may vary from the original edition.

Set in 16 pt. Plantin by Warren S. Doersam.

Printed in the United States on permanent paper.

Library of Congress Cataloging in Publication Data

De Kay, James T.
    Monitor : the story of the legendary Civil War Ironclad and
the man whose invention changed the course of history / James
Tertius de Kay.
      p. cm.
    Includes bibliographical references (p. 216–226)
    ISBN 0-7838-8441-9 (lg. print : hc : alk. paper)
    1. Monitor (Ironclad) 2. United States — History —
Civil War, 1861–1865 — Naval operations. I. Title.
[E595.M7D45   1998]
973.7′52—dc21   98-4978

For Bill Dunne
Réalt na Mara á seoladh abhaili

CONTENTS

PROLOGUE:
HAMPTON ROADS, VIRGINIA

Ships of war are, by their nature, expendable. They are temporary things, built to perform dangerous and very often difficult missions, and then to be quickly forgotten.

One of the very rare exceptions to this rule is the USS *Monitor*, the doughty little Civil War ironclad whose fame endures to this day. In her own time, she was hailed as a mechanical marvel, a milestone in the history of technology. She was for many years the best-known warship in the world, and even today she remains the most famous of all American warships. Millions of citizens with only a casual interest in matters maritime can instantly identify her distinctive "cheesebox on a raft" silhouette, a design so elegantly minimalistic it might have come off a Bauhaus drawing board.

She was the first modern battleship, the ship that changed forever the way wars were fought at sea, with a design so original it was said to include more than forty patentable innovations. Her influence on naval warfare and the design of other warships was palpable. For the previous three hundred years, the fate of nations had been decided by huge, lumbering ships of the line, great clumsy square riggers carrying up to 120 guns and manned by enormous crews of anywhere from five hundred to twelve hundred men. Then, on the morning of March 9, 1862, in the course of a brief but violent engagement in the waters of Hampton Roads, Virginia, the nimble little *Monitor*, armed with only two eleven-inch Dahlgrens, and manned by a crew of only fifty-eight men, relegated every ship of the line to the scrap heap and established an entirely new set of priorities for the navies of the world.

For all her renown, certain misconceptions still cling to the *Monitor*, the most persistent of which is the notion that she was the world's first ironclad warship, which is not even remotely the case. Both the French and the British navies had launched armor-plated warships prior to the construction of the *Monitor*, and the little Confederate navy, with only a fraction of the resources available to the Union navy, nevertheless managed to put ironclads into service long before the Yankees got around to it. Even the U.S. Army, not usually perceived to be in the vanguard of nautical development, placed an order for a squadron of ironclads for use on the Mississippi before the U.S. Navy's contract for the *Monitor* was let.

While the *Monitor* was unquestionably the most highly advanced fighting ship of her day, her very sophistication has given rise to another misconception, namely, that her fame is due more to her mechanical design than to her combat record — that she is notable more for what she was than for what she did. Such a perception ignores a number of important aspects of the *Monitor*'s story, including the vital strategic importance of her confrontation with the Confederate *Merrimac* (more properly, the CSS *Virginia*), the significant diplomatic and political consequences riding on the battle, how the complicated geography of Hampton Roads influenced the action, and not least, how the exquisite timing of the *Monitor*'s arrival at the battle site helped ensure her subsequent immortality. Only by taking into account such factors is it possible to assess how profoundly important the *Monitor* was, how great was her impact on the war, and in consequence, to understand why she remains so famous all these many years later.

If you drive down the Eastern Shore of Maryland toward the Virginia Capes, you enter the Old Confederacy by way of that remarkable engineering complex, the ten-mile-long Chesapeake Bay Bridge and Tunnel. From there, by way of the ring road that skirts the Norfolk-Portsmouth complex, you come to Interstate 664, a short feeder line that doubles back north across the waters of Hampton Roads via another combination bridge and tunnel, the Monitor-Merrimac Memorial. As the name suggests, that structure passes directly across the battle site — the bridge portion arching over it, and the tunnel portion burrowing beneath it. The top of the bridge provides an unobstructed view of Hampton Roads and its surroundings, and it is from here that you can begin to get some idea of the uniquely intimate scale of the famous battle that took place in these waters. Glancing east, you can easily pick out Sewell's Point, Old Point Comfort, and Fort Monroe, and to the west, the mouths of the Nansemond and James Rivers — the one small, the other huge. Despite the heavy industrialization of the area over the past century, the landmarks correspond precisely to the old Civil War charts. You are looking at virtually the same stretch of water and the same shoreline that existed at the time of the battle.

Halfway across the Roads, the bridge portion banks to the left and turns itself into a tunnel, and it is as your car starts its descent into the casement that you may experience a frisson of recognition as you find yourself going underwater at almost precisely the point where the *Cumberland* and the *Congress* met their fates in the tumultuous events of March 8–9, 1862.

Hampton Roads is unique among Civil War battle sites. There is a unity, a compactness to it that gives it an almost theatrical immediacy. Everything is right there in front of you, and it takes almost no effort to imagine what it must have been like that long-ago Sunday morning in 1862. Here stood ten thousand blue-coated

Union soldiers crowding the shore at Newport News, and across the Roads, another ten thousand cheering rebel troops stood gathered at Sewell's Point and Craney Island. All eyes were focused on the waters between, where two extraordinary-looking vessels, unlike anything ever seen before on earth, and each one carrying with her the hopes and ambitions of the nation that built her, moved steadily toward each other to commence the battle that would forever change the course of naval warfare.

The rest is history.

1

Toward a "Sub-Aquatic System of Naval Warfare"

The Battle of Waterloo, in 1815, marked not only the end of Napoleon's ambitions for world domination but also the beginning of the end of a kind of warfare that had changed little since the introduction of gunpowder into Europe in the thirteenth century. For five hundred years following that epochal development, military leaders had been banging away at each other in increasingly predictable fashion, employing strategies barely refined since the days of their great-grandfathers. But even as the squadron of Royal Navy vessels squared away for the South Atlantic to deposit the defeated Bonaparte at his final home on St. Helena, invisible historical forces were already beginning to reshape the world, and would soon radically transform everything in it, including the means by which armies and navies went about the business of waging war.

14

The great unseen impetus for change was that momentous confluence of political, scientific, and commercial crosscurrents now known as the Industrial Revolution, which had been slowly maturing for decades in the "dark satanic mills" crowding the riverbanks of Europe, and which had recently been quickened into new life by a number of seminal developments, the most important of which was James Watt's improved steam engine. With the return of peace after Waterloo, Great Britain, the first country to benefit from Watt's new engines, emerged unchallenged as the world's leading industrial power. The City of London became the financial and entrepreneurial center of the new technological economy, drawing to it venture capitalists, inventors, and visionaries eager to profit from the new opportunities for wealth.

It was an extraordinarily dynamic era, both stimulating and unsettling, as new ideas arose to challenge conventional wisdom, and new ways of doing things came into conflict with long-established patterns of thought and behavior. It was into this world of change, in the spring of 1826, that a young, twenty-three-year-old Swedish engineer named John Ericsson arrived in London, eager to carve out a career as an inventor. Ericsson, an intense, ambitious, and at times obsessive perfectionist, would become a major contributor to the technological dynamism of his era, most notably in the field of naval warfare. His most significant achievement would be the USS

Monitor. Over the next thirty-six years, he would dream up her original concept, personally design every one of her unique features, and eventually, after countless frustrations and disappointments, see his vision triumphantly realized.

Ericsson was born in 1803 in the remote Swedish village of Långbanshyttan, in the province of Värmland. He was recognized from an early age as a prodigy, and his father, a mining engineer, encouraged the boy. By the age of five, he had already invented a working windmill built from the springs and gears of an old clock augmented by bits of tableware borrowed from his mother. When Ericsson was eight years old, his father took a job as a supervisor on the construction of the Göta Canal, an ambitious engineering project designed to span the entire width of Sweden. At the family's new home at Forsvik, the boy received a solid, if informal, education from some of the other engineers on the project, including instruction in English, French, Latin, and chemistry, as well as architectural and mechanical drawing. Eventually he went to work for his father and rose quickly to the position of assistant surveyor, despite the fact that he was still too short to reach the eyepiece of his leveling instrument without the aid of a stoop carried by an assistant. At sixteen, he was put in charge of a crew of six hundred men and was made responsible for drawing up plans for the entire canal and for the care and maintenance of all the machinery and tools used in its construction.

The following year, in 1820, the young Ericsson joined the army, where he was set to work preparing maps of the military areas in and around Jamtland, near the arctic circle. When his maps were forwarded to Stockholm, they were instantly recognized as cartographic masterpieces. They are still extant today, carefully preserved in the Swedish Royal Archives.

The army gave Ericsson the opportunity to practice his other engineering skills as well, including the design of steam engines, primarily for draining ditches. While involved in this project, it occurred to him that if he could use hot air to run the engines, rather than steam, he could vastly improve their efficiency. His experiments along this line eventually resulted in what he called his "flame engine," which, in a demonstration before the Swedish Engineering Society in Stockholm, produced ten horsepower. While the flame engine offered considerable promise, Sweden was a poor country, with only limited opportunities for exploiting the design, and Ericsson was encouraged to take his invention to England, where the bankers of Lombard Street stood ready to support almost any promising form of industrial innovation. When the British minister in Stockholm arranged for him to speak before the Society of Civil Engineers in London, the young officer, filled with ambition and dreams of success, packed his bag, borrowed a thousand crowns, and set sail for England. He would never see his native land again.

Ericsson arrived in London with a working model of his flame engine, which he claimed was considerably more efficient than any steam engine then on the market, but alas, when it came time to demonstrate it before an audience of fellow engineers, his engine, which had worked so well at home where wood was the basic fuel, proved unadaptable to British coal, and Ericsson was forced to set it aside for further tinkering.

Undaunted, he established a partnership with an English engineer named John Braithwaite and quickly began making a name for himself as a clever and resourceful — if somewhat willful — designer of ventilating systems, fire pumps, and railway locomotives, a man who could turn his hand to almost any mechanical problem and come up with a practical, and often elegant, solution.

Examined today, Ericsson's drawings still exhibit a singular purity of style. Even with the most mundane project, he strove for simplicity and took pains to eliminate everything that was not essential. The beauty and superior workmanship of Ericsson's designs did not go unnoticed. His railroad locomotive, the *Novelty*, which he conceived and built from scratch in just seven weeks in 1829 for a contest sponsored by the Liverpool & Manchester Railway, was as highly praised for its style as for its performance. The *Times* reported that "the *Novelty* was the lightest and most elegant carriage on the road yesterday, and the velocity with which it moved surprised and amazed every beholder." A writer for the *Mechanics Magazine* was equally complimentary, noting that "the great lightness of the *Novelty*, its great compactness, its beautiful workmanship, excited universal admiration."

In one test, the *Novelty* covered a measured mile in fifty-three seconds, establishing a new land speed record, but beauty and superior engineering turned out to be insufficient to win that particular contest. The sponsors, who wanted another entrant to win, changed the rules in the middle of the competition in an effort to eliminate the foreigner Ericsson and subsequently disqualified his entry on a technicality. The incident undoubtedly fed the inventor's inherent distrust of the English.

Ericsson had arrived in Britain with no particular background or interest in shipbuilding, but like most entrepreneurial types he was an opportunist. When he saw the great significance that the English attached to naval construction, and the liberal financial rewards to be garnered by those who produced what the Royal Navy wanted, he made it his business to find out as much as he could about such matters. He quickly realized that the highly specialized world of warship design was in the throes of a momentous upheaval as a result of two recent but unrelated advances in maritime technology. The first such advance was the increasing reliability of marine steam engines, which was bringing about the first major redesign of warships since the development of square rigging. The second was the recent introduction of a new, infinitely more destructive kind of artillery called the shell gun. It was Ericsson's efforts to create a warship incorporating both steam power and the shell gun that led directly to his design of the *Monitor*.

Shell guns had been developed in France under the direction of Colonel Henri-Joseph Paixhans, a veteran of Napoleon's artillery corps. They were large-caliber cannon that fired hollow explosive projectiles filled with gunpowder, instead of the traditional solid iron shot. The projectiles were known as "shells" because their metal casings enclosed the explosive charge in the same way that rigid seashells and eggshells encase their contents. The shells were detonated by metal fuses and could be set to explode on or after impact. Colonel Paixhans advocated arming naval vessels with his new guns and predicted that sea battles would no longer be decided by the familiar iron cannonballs that buried themselves in ships' timbers or bounced off their oaken hulls, but by his new shells, which would penetrate the wooden walls and explode, tearing gaping holes in the side of the target vessels, setting them on fire, and inevitably sinking them.

Paixhans guns were still in the experimental stage, and had yet to be tested in combat, but in supervised trials, in which shells were fired into target casements built to the strength and dimensions of a ship's gunwales, it was clearly demonstrated that the guns had the potential to destroy any wooden naval vessel afloat — a matter of some moment, given that every last naval vessel in the world was built of wood.

The young Ericsson studied the threat posed by the Paixhans guns and proposed a solution that was characteristically straightforward and uncompromising: If shell guns could destroy wooden ships, he reasoned, then wooden ships were by definition obsolete. In the future, Ericsson argued, naval vessels would have to be protected by enough iron armor to withstand the fire of the shell guns.

The idea of building ships out of iron was not in itself particularly revolutionary. There were already a number of merchant vessels constructed of iron in service at the time Ericsson made his suggestion, notably the *Aaron Manby*. But Ericsson was advocating something far more difficult to achieve than simply the use of iron as a building material. He wanted to use it as a protective armor plate. The difference between an iron ship, such as the *Aaron Manby*, and an ironclad ship, such as Ericsson proposed, was, to use a modern analogy, the difference between an automobile and an armored tank. Both were built from the same materials, but in fundamentally different ways, and for fundamentally different purposes.

While the use of ironcladding was not common at the time, neither was it entirely unknown. As early as the third century B.C., the king of Syracuse was reported to have armor-plated a merchant vessel by sheathing it in lead, and in 1592 the Korean admiral Yi-sun had repelled a Japanese naval attack with an ironclad "tortoise ship." As recently as the 1780s, the Spanish had employed floating gun batteries protected by sheet iron.

Not everyone shared Ericsson's faith in ironcladding. Skeptics argued that earlier ironclad vessels required only limited amounts of sheathing to resist attack, but that cannon were now so powerful that a ship would require armor plate at least two inches thick for adequate protection. So much additional weight would vastly increase a vessel's instability, it was argued, and create a slew of troublesome design problems relating to speed and seaworthiness. Opponents of ironcladding pointed out, moreover, that the fuses used to detonate Colonel Paixhans's projectiles were notoriously untrustworthy, suggesting that the danger posed by the French guns was in all likelihood overrated.

Ericsson vehemently disagreed. As an engineer, he knew from experience that it was almost always a simple matter to correct a mechanical problem once it was defined. He argued adamantly that it was time to begin experimenting with ironcladding before gunnery experts remedied the problems in Paixhans's fuses. But no one in naval circles was as yet ready to pay much attention to the unsolicited advice of a young and untried Swedish mechanic. As a result, the navies of the world chose to ignore the threat and, for the time being, continued to build their ships of oak.

The other development influencing warship design, the increasing reliability of marine steam engines, was an equally significant harbinger of change. Steam had long been employed successfully in commercial vessels, beginning with Robert Fulton's *Clermont* in 1807, but in the 1820s its use in warships was still limited. Naval officers understood and appreciated the potential importance of steam — they were particularly excited by the fact that it gave them the ability to choose their battle positions in combat regardless of wind or weather, an enormous tactical advantage — but Admiralty shipwrights were quick to point out that for all the advantages of steam, the inherent drawbacks appeared to outweigh the potential benefits.

The most obvious problem lay in the prodigious quantities of fuel required to keep a steamship in motion. Steam engines consumed far more coal than a warship could possibly carry on a long voyage, a fact that made them of use only in specialized vessels, such as harbor tugs, river packets, and coasters, the kind of ships that never strayed far from a coaling station.

In an attempt to combine the advantages of

steam with the practicality of sail, navies experimented with compromise vessels — sailing ships with auxiliary steam engines — with indifferent results, primarily because there was still another serious problem with steamers that bore directly on their fighting qualities, namely, the vulnerability of their means of propulsion.

The only practical way that had as yet been devised to move steamships through the water was with large and clumsy paddlewheels, usually mounted amidships on either side of the vessel. In order to function properly, both the wheels and the machinery to operate them had to be located above the waterline, where they were easy targets for enemy guns. A single well-placed shot could disable a paddlewheel and render a ship helpless. For that reason alone, it was generally acknowledged among shipbuilders that for all the promise of steam, sail was not only superior but, barring some unforeseen change in circumstances, would likely remain so.

As an engineer, Ericsson harbored an innate bias for steam over sail, but he had no immediate solution to either the problem of excessive fuel consumption or the vulnerability of paddlewheels. At some point in the second half of 1826, a vague notion for a new kind of steam warship started to take shape in the back of his mind, a concept he would subsequently label, with somewhat ponderous solemnity, his "sub-aquatic system of naval warfare."

Ericsson, usually a meticulous record keeper, was never entirely clear as to the precise details of his sub-aquatic system, particularly in its earliest formulations. But in essence, he seems to have envisioned an invincible steam-powered warship that would be shot- and shell-proof, in part because it was ironclad, and in part because its means of propulsion would be located safely below the ship's waterline, and therefore beyond the reach of enemy guns.

The sub-aquatic system was a straightforward enough concept as far as it went, save for the fact that neither John Ericsson nor anyone else had the remotest idea how to build it — the technology simply did not exist. Over the next quarter century, sandwiching his efforts between more remunerative engineering projects, he sought to develop such a technology.

His first priority was to devise some method of propelling a steamship through water other than by paddlewheel. It took Ericsson several years to work out a solution, but finally, by 1837, he had his answer. It was his screw propeller, the first practical, modern propeller, the direct ancestor of the propellers used in virtually every motorized vessel in the world today. At a single stroke, Ericsson's screw propeller not only significantly increased the efficiency of the steam engine but, more important in terms of warship design, relocated the means of propulsion underwater, out of harm's way.

As a means of promoting his invention,

Ericsson built a tugboat, the *Francis P. Ogden,* which featured his new propeller, and launched it with great fanfare on the Thames on April 19, 1837. In her first trial the boat exceeded ten knots, and was quickly dubbed the "Flying Devil." A triumphant Ericsson, hoping to win a fat contract from the Royal Navy, arranged to have the "Flying Devil" tow the lords of the Admiralty in their barge from Somerset House to Blackburn and back. On this occasion the tugboat actually exceeded its previous ten-knot record, but their lordships were unenthusiastic. Sir William Symonds, surveyor of the Royal Navy, dismissed the invention as impractical. "Even if the screw has the power to propel a vessel," he explained airily, "it would be found altogether useless in practice because, the power being applied at the stern, it would be absolutely impossible to make the vessel steer." The touchy and thin-skinned Ericsson took the rejection to heart. He suspected, possibly with cause, that the English held his nationality against him. His abiding distrust of the British — stemming from what he believed was their mistrust of him — undoubtedly played a part in his decision in 1839 to abandon London and move across the Atlantic to New York. It was there that he would solve the remaining problems relating to his sub-aquatic system.

Ericsson came to the United States at the urging of an American naval officer named Robert

F. Stockton, who had "discovered" the Swedish engineer in London and been impressed by his energy and vision. Stockton was a man of independent wealth and considerable political influence and was eager to have Ericsson design ships for the U.S. Navy. But at the time of Ericsson's arrival, Stockton's political clout was temporarily on the wane due to a change of parties in Washington, and he was not immediately able to obtain the contract he sought. For a time, Ericsson was forced to fend for himself. He soon managed to drum up interest in his screw propeller, and within three years he had five propeller craft operating, two on the Great Lakes and three on the Chesapeake and Delaware Canal.

Finally, in 1842, Robert Stockton's political star was once again in the ascendant, and he was able at last to arrange for Ericsson to design and supervise the construction of an experimental corvette for the navy. She was built in Philadelphia and was eventually christened the *Princeton*, in honor of Stockton's birthplace, in New Jersey. She was immediately hailed as an engineering triumph and was greatly admired in naval circles on both sides of the Atlantic. Many of her innovative features would eventually be incorporated in the *Monitor*, including forced air blowers and furnaces that burned anthracite coal for greater efficiency. The ship was designed around Ericsson's screw propeller and was powered by a radically new steam engine of his design that was powerful enough to move the ship at high speed yet compact enough to fit easily into the bottom of the hull, completely below the waterline. With both the engine and the means of propulsion thus shielded from enemy guns, the basic elements of his sub-aquatic system were at last in place. To be sure, the *Princeton* did not incorporate the full system — she was built of wood, for one thing, instead of iron, and she carried a full set of sails, like any ordinary warship of the day. But to anyone who understood naval architecture, she represented a radical break with the past.

The *Princeton* exceeded all expectations in terms of speed, maneuverability, and firepower. Her main battery, a huge twelve-inch gun that had been designed by Ericsson prior to his departure from England and cast under his supervision at the Mersey Iron Works, near Liverpool, was recognized as a highly significant achievement in naval ordnance. Ericsson christened his gun the Orator, because, he said, it was intended to speak with authority. (The name was later changed to the Oregon, in part to downplay its British origins.) The gun was so powerful it could fire a 225-pound projectile five miles with unequaled accuracy and could penetrate fifty-seven inches of oak timber, or four inches of wrought iron, all of which made the *Princeton* the most formidable naval vessel in the world.

Stockton, who had aspirations as an engineer himself, designed a companion gun that he arranged to have mounted in the place of honor, on the forecastle, while Ericsson's gun was relegated to the quarterdeck. Stockton's gun, which he christened Peacemaker, was the same caliber as Ericsson's, but he had decided it was unnecessary to follow the Swede's cautious example of strengthening the breech with transverse banding. On the occasion of a private demonstration before a distinguished group of guests during the ship's inaugural visit to Washington, Stockton's gun exploded and burst at the breech, killing eight onlookers, including the secretary of state, the secretary of the navy, and Colonel David Gardiner of New York, the father of President John Tyler's fiancée. In the resulting scandal, Stockton managed to shift the blame to the innocent Ericsson and then used his political weight to see to it that Ericsson was never paid for his work in designing and building the *Princeton*. Over the next several years, Ericsson tried time and again to clear his name and get the money due him, without success.

Interestingly, one of his staunchest champions in Washington during the years of controversy and counterclaims was Stephen Mallory, a senator from Florida and chairman of the Naval Affairs Committee, who frequently took the engineer's side against the navy. Years later, Mallory would become the Confederate secretary of the navy.

In the years following the *Princeton* disaster, Ericsson was kept busy in the courts of law, suing the navy to recover his costs, and also as a means of protecting himself against industrial pirates who were blithely ignoring his patents on his increasingly popular screw propeller. In 1846 and 1847, he involved himself in some relatively unimportant government work, first designing a theoretical ironclad for the House Committee on Naval Affairs, and then advising the Treasury Department on the design of its revenue cutters.

On October 28, 1848, Ericsson took out U.S. citizenship, a circumstance in which he always took considerable pride. It was around this time that he also returned to his first love, his flame engine, which he had now rechristened the "caloric engine." He was pleased to discover the small versions of his invention found a ready market and soon provided him with a modest but regular income. Then, in 1851, having become convinced that a large caloric engine was equally practicable, he persuaded a group of Wall Street capitalists to finance the construction of a 260-foot-long merchant ship powered by his caloric engines, which was christened the *Ericsson*. Because he wanted the ship to be a showcase for his caloric engines, and did not want the public confused by any other aspect of her performance, he deliberately designed her as a paddlewheeler, rather than a propeller-driven vessel. In a trial against a steam-powered competitor, the *Ericsson* made ten knots and could not match the steamer's sixteen knots, but she proved to be vastly more economical to run, consuming only six tons of coal in twenty-four hours, as against the competition's fifty-eight tons. Horace Greeley, of the *New York Tribune*, announced that "the age of steam is closed, the age of caloric opens. Fulton and Watt belong to the past. Ericsson is the great mechanical genius of the present and future."

And then once again, on the cusp of his latest success, disaster struck. On April 27, 1854, in a freak storm, the *Ericsson* foundered off the New Jersey coast. Although she was later successfully recovered, the financiers who had bankrolled her, and therefore owned her, insisted on replacing her experimental engines with conventional steam. For Ericsson, it was another bitter disappointment.

But by that time, the inventor's attention was once again diverted by an opportunity to build his "sub-aquatic system of naval warfare." Halfway around the world, war had broken out between Russia and Turkey in the Crimea.

In the first weeks of that war, on November 30, 1853, a Russian naval squadron of six sailing ships and three steamers, all built of wood, caught up with a Turkish squadron of nine sailing ships and two steamers, also built of wood, lying at anchor in the little harbor of Sinope, on the Black Sea. The Russian ships were equipped with shell guns, while the Turks had only iron shot. In a short but devastating action, the Russians' exploding shells cut the Turks to pieces, with a frightful loss of lives. Ten of the eleven Turkish vessels were either sunk or captured, and only one managed to escape. Russian losses were negligible.

The massacre at Sinope was news around the world, and its basic lesson — that wooden ships were powerless to resist shell guns — was duly noted by everyone concerned with the construction of naval vessels. In New York, John Ericsson read the reports of the battle with intense interest. As a native of Sweden, he was distressed that his homeland's historic enemy, the detested Russians, should have gained the victory, but as an engineer, he was pleased that the evidence was so unequivocal. Here, finally, was clear documentation of the devastating effect of the Paixhans shell guns against wooden hulls. When France and Britain came into the war on the side of the Ottoman Empire, Ericsson decided the time was propitious to strike a blow against the Russians, and to offer his "sub-aquatic system of naval warfare" to the world. As a result of his years in London, he still mistrusted the English, so he decided to try to interest French emperor Louis Napoleon in his warship.

On September 26, 1854, after several months of intense creative effort directed toward refining his vision and getting it down on paper, Ericsson submitted to the French government, through the Swedish consul in New York, a full set of plans for his invincible shot- and shell-proof man-of-war.

The actual plans have long since disappeared, but a copy of Ericsson's covering letter to the emperor remains, and its description of the vessel confirms that she was in large measure the same ship the world would one day recognize as the *Monitor*. Reading the description today, one can still sense the almost childlike enthusiasm Ericsson had for the project.

"The vessel [is] to be composed entirely of iron," he begins unequivocally, as if to dispel any possible confusion on that most basic point. "The midship section is triangular, with a broad, hollow keel, loaded with about 200 tons of cast-iron blocks to balance the heavy upper works. The ends of the vessel are moderately sharp." Then, "The deck, made of plate iron, is curved both longitudinally and transversely, the curvature being 5 feet." Here we see where the search for a sub-aquatic system has finally led Ericsson. The vessel, like an iceberg, is now almost entirely submerged. Not only are the engines, steering mechanism, and means of propulsion under water, but so is virtually the whole ship — including living quarters and workstations for most of the crew. The deck, only a portion of which is above the surface, has become the top of the vessel, a fortified shield that "is covered with a lining of sheet iron 3 inches thick." The deck extends out beyond the hull on all sides, like the flight deck of a modern aircraft carrier, and because it curves downward, the edges actually lie below water level. Ericsson assures the emperor that "shot striking the deck are deflected, whilst shell exploding on it will prove harmless."

Another defensive measure: The deck "is made to project 8 feet over the rudder and propeller." In other words, not only will the motive power and steering be under water, but they will be protected by an iron umbrella, overlapping the sides and end of the vessel.

Only a small part of the ship was to ride above the waterline, but this turned out to be one of the ship's most important features, described by Ericsson as "a semi-globular turret of plate 6 inches thick revolving on a vertical column by means of steam power and appropriate gear work." The turret, which housed the vessel's main armament, was not to be the cylindrical "cheesebox" associated with the *Monitor* but a "globular" hemisphere, more like a half grapefruit resting upside down on a plate. Because the ship had no masts and no funnel, the turret could traverse a full 360 degrees and fire in any direction without endangering or injuring the ship. Ericsson never took credit for inventing the turret — he said the idea went back to the ancient Greeks — but it would prove to be one of the most important, and most copied, features of the *Monitor*.

Both the "sub-aquatic" crew and the various steam engines that powered the ship and the turret would require constant supplies of fresh air, and Ericsson described how he planned to provide it. "Air for the combustion in the boilers and for ventilation within the vessel is supplied by a large self-acting centrifugal blower, the fresh air being drawn in through numerous small holes in the turret. The products of combustion in the boilers and the impure air from the vessel are forced out by conductors leading to a cluster of small holes in the deck and turret."

Visibility would of necessity be highly limited, but the captain and those members of the crew who needed to see what was going on in surrounding waters would use periscopes, or, as he describes them, "reflecting telescopes, capable of being protruded or withdrawn at pleasure."

Perhaps the most startling innovations of Ericsson's proto-*Monitor* were its two major weapons. The turret was to be fitted with a single — and very singular — gun, so unlike any other that the inventor refers to it neither as a gun nor as a cannon, but as a "tube for projecting the shells." It is "to be made of cast iron or brass, 20 inches bore, 2 inches thick, and 10 feet long. It is open at one end, the other end being closed by a door moving on hinges provided with a cross-bar and set-screw, in order to be quickly opened and afterwards firmly secured. The shell is inserted through this door, and projected by the direct action of steam admitted from the boiler of the vessel through a large opening at the breech." In other words, this was an entirely new kind of artillery, not fired by gunpowder but pro-

jected by jets of steam pressure, a steam gun —
and a breech-loading steam gun at that!

In addition to the steam gun in the turret,
another unique weapon system was built into the
ship below the waterline, in the form of a pair of
permanently mounted tubes, one on either side
of the vessel. These tubes were to fire ten-foot-
long underwater projectiles equipped with explosive heads and referred to by the inventor as
"hydrostatic javelins." Today we would call them
torpedoes. Like the projectiles fired from the turret, the hydrostatic javelins were also to be propelled by steam.

As it turned out, the French emperor, or more
likely his chief naval adviser, Dupuy de Lôme,
who was already experimenting with ironclad batteries, did not share Ericsson's enthusiasm. In
due course, the inventor received a courteous
note from Paris, written by someone in the emperor's office, acknowledging receipt of his plans.
"The Emperor himself has examined with great
care the new system of naval attack that you have
submitted to him," the note informed him, and
then in a polite but cool rebuff indicated that the
emperor and his staff did not find "the result to
be obtained would be proportionate to the ex-
pense or to the small number of guns that could
be brought into use."

And so it was not to be in the Crimea that
Ericsson's visionary warship would receive its
baptism of fire. The disappointed inventor put

aside his drawings and tossed his little cardboard model into a box. There it was to remain for almost another decade, until the election of Abraham Lincoln as president of the United States in November 1860 set in motion the chain of events that would finally lead to the realization of John Ericsson's "sub-aquatic system of naval warfare."

2

THE LOSS OF THE
MERRIMAC

The months between Lincoln's election and his
inauguration were to be crucial to the subsequent
history of John Ericsson's visionary ironclad.
While the little model of the ship continued to
gather dust in his house at 36 Beach Street in
New York, the shifting political crisis in Washington was establishing the specific circumstances
that would eventually make the construction of
the actual vessel virtually inevitable.

Under the lame-duck leadership of President
James Buchanan, the federal government studi-
ously avoided any actions that might provoke
the increasingly bellicose secessionist states,
and as a result, by March 4, 1861, when the
new administration took office, it was already
too late for Lincoln or his cabinet to affect the
shape of events. The new president concen-
trated his efforts on trying to hold the remaining slave states in the Union, while
simultaneously seeking accommodation with

those states that had already left.

But while Lincoln continued to search for peace, his newly installed administration had to prepare for war. Across the street from the White House, Lincoln's new secretary of the navy, Gideon Welles, found himself overwhelmed by his new duties. Welles was a newspaperman from Hartford, Connecticut, and had been selected for his position primarily because Lincoln felt the need for someone from New England in his cabinet. He had little in his background to prepare him for the awesome complexity of his new responsibilities, but he had a keen mind and was a quick study, and it did not take him long to discover that the U.S. Navy was in no condition to fight a war of any kind, certainly not the major war that many now saw as inevitable.

The United States was one of the leading maritime nations in the world, with almost six thousand miles of coastline, a number of flourishing seaports on two oceans, and significant trade commitments overseas. To fulfill its commercial obligations, it maintained a merchant fleet that was second in size only to Great Britain's. Yet in spite of its significant presence on the open seas, the United States had never sought a navy commensurate with its size and prominence, and had chosen instead to maintain a minimal naval service with only a few ships and a small officer corps. The country was now about to pay a steep price for its lack of preparedness.

In the months since the election, many of the navy's most valuable officers had resigned their commissions and "gone South" to offer their services to the Confederacy, and of those who remained, too many were overage and out of touch. The senior ranks were made up almost exclusively of superannuated veterans of the War of 1812, who were totally inexperienced in any of the aspects of naval warfare that had emerged since that time.

The navy's ships were in just as bad shape as the personnel. The fleet, much of it scattered around the world on foreign assignment, consisted of only forty-two vessels in commission, most of them obsolete sailing vessels, and virtually all of them unsuited to the blockade service that Welles knew Lincoln was contemplating. The job of setting the navy on a wartime footing was going to be a long and arduous effort, he recognized, one that would entail a huge program of recruitment, training, purchase, and construction.

On April 10, 1861, just two days before the Confederate bombardment of Fort Sumter ushered in the war, Welles found himself involved in a particularly delicate problem involving the Norfolk Navy Yard, in Virginia. As it turned out, his inadvertent mishandling of the situation, brought on by his inexperience, resulted in a major disaster for the navy and provided the South with the very weapon that would make the *Monitor* necessary.

The Norfolk Navy Yard was the largest and best-equipped shipyard in the country, located in Gosport, Virginia, directly across the Elizabeth River from the city of Norfolk and twelve miles upriver from the magnificent harbor of Hampton Roads. On April 10, the state of Virginia was still nominally loyal to the Union, but just how long it might remain so was a matter of nervous conjecture among the leaders in Washington. Virginia was a slave state, and there was every reason to believe that it might, at any moment, decide to join the newly formed Confederacy. Should that situation arise, it would be extremely difficult for the navy to defend the yard, which would almost certainly fall into rebel hands.

The navy yard would make a spectacularly valuable prize. It was equipped with extensive modern construction facilities, including a huge granite dry dock and numerous warehouses and storage buildings crammed with cannon, gunpowder, shells, cannonballs, and small arms, as well as rope, timber, machinery, tools, steam engines, and other valuable naval stores.

In addition, there were twelve warships berthed at Norfolk, including three sailing sloops, four ships of the line, and three sailing frigates. By far the most valuable vessel in the collection was the USS *Merrimac*, a sleek, powerful, 4,636-ton combination steam and sailing frigate, carrying forty guns; she was recognized as one of the most modern and powerful warships in the world. Although christened *Merrimack* in 1854, she had somehow managed to lose the *k* at the end of her name in the intervening years, and she was almost universally referred to by the abbreviated spelling, even in official documents.*

The *Merrimac* had recently returned from a tour of duty in the Orient and was now laid up "in ordinary" at Norfolk, awaiting repairs, her guns unshipped, her engines dismantled and condemned.

The commandant of the yard, Commodore Charles S. McCauley, was an officer of more than fifty years' service, somewhat enfeebled, and much given to drink. He was a Pennsylvanian, and therefore presumably loyal to the Union, but the Navy Department in Washington was well aware that most of the officers under his command were either Virginians or suspected Southern sympathizers. It was impossible to replace them as long as Virginia remained in the Union, but there was every reason to believe that in the event of war they might try to keep the *Merrimac* at Norfolk until she could be turned over to the Confederacy.

It was to forestall such a possibility that an anxious Gideon Welles addressed a confidential letter to the commandant at Norfolk. Welles had a keen mind, but he had not been in office long

---

* A similar orthographic confusion still seems to afflict those citizens of northeastern Massachusetts who live in the village of Merrimac, on the banks of the Merrimack River.

enough to understand the need for absolute clarity in any orders emanating from his desk. The letter began by stating its purpose with a commendable lack of ambiguity.

SIR: In view of the peculiar condition of the country, and of events that have already transpired, it becomes necessary that great vigilance should be exercised in guarding and protecting the public interests and property committed to your charge. It is therefore deemed important that the steamer *Merrimac* should be in condition to proceed to Philadelphia or to any other yard, should it be deemed necessary, or, in case of danger from unlawful attempts to take possession of her, that she may be placed beyond their reach.

Indeed, it is desirable that all the shipping and stores should be attended to, and should you think an additional force necessary, or that other precautions are required, you will immediately apprise the Department. In the meantime exercise your own judgment in discharging the responsibility that devolves on you.

If Welles had closed his letter there, he might have saved himself — and the entire Union cause — a good deal of grief. Instead, he appended some additional details, including a phrase that, while seemingly innocuous, in fact added an entirely new gloss to his directive: "It is desirable that there should be no steps taken to give needless alarm."

The phrase created an ambiguity in the secretary's order. In effect, it gave the commandant a free hand. If he judged that any of the steps outlined in the first part of the letter might give "needless alarm," he could disregard them. Welles unwittingly handed over the responsibility for a critical decision to an old man who drank too much, and who was surrounded by suspected traitors.

Almost as soon as the directive was sent on its way, news reached Washington of the bombardment of Fort Sumter. The long-threatened war was now a reality, and the removal of the *Merrimac* became a matter of pressing importance. She had to be got out of Norfolk immediately and moved, if possible, to Philadelphia. McCauley had already informed Welles that she was in a state of such disrepair it would take at least a month to make her ready for sea, but the Union no longer had a month to spare. Besides, Welles suspected the commandant's estimate was based on deliberately falsified information from McCauley's disloyal subordinates. He dispatched Commander James Alden and the navy's chief engineer, Benjamin Isherwood, to Norfolk with orders to survey the situation and get the *Merrimac* out to sea as quickly as humanly possible, either under her own power or, failing that, under tow.

On Saturday, April 13, Alden disembarked at the city of Norfolk to learn that news of his impending arrival had preceded him, and that his supposedly secret orders were common knowledge. Shaken by this discovery, and concerned by the openly expressed sympathy for the Confederate cause that he encountered on every side, he made his way across the river to the navy yard and the commandant's office, where he learned of an even more distressing turn of events: The entire civilian workforce at the yard had resigned and gone home. The next morning, a Sunday, Chief Engineer Isherwood joined Alden at the empty yard and immediately set about examining the *Merrimac*'s engines, which had been totally dismantled, with the parts scattered throughout the yard. He quickly ascertained that the engines were in better shape than McCauley's messages had indicated, and estimated it would take only three days to get them working well enough to move the ship at least the few miles downriver to Hampton Roads, where, protected by the Union guns at Fort Monroe, she would be safe from rebel seizure. The two men scouted the area for mechanics to handle the repairs, and with the promise of generous bonuses, they eventually assembled enough men to do the job. Isherwood set up an around-the-clock work schedule and dispatched a coded message to Welles reporting the ship would be ready to move on April 18. On receipt of the telegraphed message, Welles ordered Commodore Hiram Paulding to join Alden and Isherwood in Norfolk specifically to handle McCauley, who was sending one message after another complaining about the two men sent down from Washington and otherwise making a nuisance of himself.

While the navy sought to save the *Merrimac*, other events were impinging on the situation at Norfolk. On April 15, in direct response to the fall of Fort Sumter, President Lincoln put out a call for seventy-five thousand volunteers "to repossess the forts, places and properties which have been seized." The president's proclamation called for every state still in the Union, including Virginia, to provide a proportion of the overall levy. This demand on the part of Washington finally forced the legislature in Richmond, which had been procrastinating for months over the question of joining the Confederacy, to face up to the choice of fighting for or against the South. Predictably, two days after Lincoln's call for volunteers, Virginia passed the secret Ordinance of Secession. Armed with the ordinance, the governor moved quickly to secure those military facilities the federal government maintained in the state, and sent the newly commissioned major general of militia, William B. Taliaferro, to Norfolk to demand the surrender of the naval base. Taliaferro, after securing a promise of reinforcement by two regiments of South Carolina infantry and four companies of Georgia militia, set off for Norfolk by train.

On the same day that the legislature in Richmond secretly took Virginia out of the Union, an exhausted Benjamin Isherwood in Norfolk completed his repairs of the *Merrimac*'s engines. At four in the afternoon, the engineer proudly informed McCauley that the ship was now in condition to leave Norfolk the following day under her own power, and he asked the commandant for permission to fire the boilers. The befuddled McCauley was startled and confused by the news. How had Isherwood and his scratch crew managed to complete a job in only a few days that his own people had assured him would take several weeks? He seemed to have trouble absorbing the information and told the engineer not to take any action until the following day.

The next morning, the *Merrimac*, with Commander Alden now in command, lay anchored off the sea-wall at the navy yard, fired up and ready to leave, pending only the permission from McCauley that Isherwood had requested the day before. Every precaution had been taken to ensure that the ship could be moved quickly in an emergency. Even the chain cables, which moored her to the dock, had been replaced by ropes, which could be severed by axes if necessary. It had been impossible to recruit a crew sufficient to take the ship to Philadelphia, but the top-ranking seagoing officer at Norfolk, Commodore Garrett J. Pendergast, who was not under the command of McCauley, had arranged for thirty sailors from his flagship *Cumberland* to be temporarily transferred to the *Merrimac*. These men, along with the forty-four firemen and coal heavers Alden had hired at inflated wages, gave him enough manpower to at least get the ship to the Union army base at Fort Monroe, situated eighteen miles distant at the mouth of Hampton Roads. In the meantime, Alden scouted around for a civilian pilot, offering a thousand dollars to the man who could get them down the river and across the tricky currents of the Roads.

The bibulous McCauley continued to delay. As the hour grew increasingly late, and the situation more desperate, he finally made his decision. Unaware that the legislature in Richmond had already taken Virginia out of the Union, and that the militia was on its way to demand surrender of the navy yard, he decided he could not take a chance that his action would force Virginia to secede. He ordered the *Merrimac*'s fires drawn and her engines shut down. Alden was beside himself with frustration but dared not countermand an order from a superior, even one who was, in Alden's words, "weak, vacillating, hesitating and overwhelmed." A bitter Isherwood returned to the *Merrimac* and carried out the commandant's orders. Then the two men, who did not want to trust news of McCauley's most recent action to the telegraph for fear the message might be intercepted, hurried off to Washington by overnight steamer to alert the secretary of the navy in person.

Gideon Welles, after hearing the report from Isherwood and Alden on Friday, April 19, finally relieved McCauley of his command and ordered Paulding, who had by this time returned to Washington, back to Norfolk with orders to defend the navy yard if possible, and if not, to destroy it and all the ships that could not be moved. Welles made it clear that Paulding's most important priority was to save the *Merrimac*, even if it was necessary to tow her out. Paulding loaded an extra forty barrels of gunpowder and eleven tanks of turpentine on board the steamer *Pawnee* and cast off from Washington late in the afternoon.

It was fortuitous that Paulding brought his own incendiaries and explosives, for on the same day he set off from Washington, General Taliaferro arrived in Norfolk, with orders to seize the navy yard. After rounding up whatever militia he could muster, he attempted to threaten the navy yard by setting up gun emplacements on the opposite bank of the river. When this failed to intimidate the handful of loyal officers in charge, he marched his men to Fort Norfolk on the east side of the river and took possession of the navy's undefended magazine, seizing 2,800 barrels of gunpowder for the Confederacy without firing a shot.

The *Pawnee* arrived at Fort Monroe the following afternoon, a Saturday, and stopped long enough to embark 349 members of the Third Massachusetts Regiment, who already had orders to defend the navy base. Toward evening, the

Pawnee fired up again and made her way across Hampton Roads and up the Elizabeth River, steaming toward Norfolk and the navy yard, where Paulding expected to find the *Merrimac* and the other vessels in the yard resting at anchor. Instead, he arrived at 8 P.M. to find a scene of carnage. Every ship assigned to the yard was either sunk or sinking in the shallow waters of the Elizabeth. Several hours earlier, he learned, McCauley had changed his mind still again and given the order to scuttle all the ships, except for the *Cumberland*, which was not under his command. Sailors had been sent into the ships with orders to open the sea valves, the water had poured in, and the entire squadron now lay on the bottom. It was an incredible sight; the *Merrimac*, in particular, careened at a crazy angle, her keel resting on the shallow bottom, her upper works and part of her hull still above water level. Appalled, Paulding sent a party into the ship to assess the damage, only to learn that it would require divers with full equipment (which they had failed to bring with them) to close the *Merrimac*'s sea cocks, and even then there was no telling how much time it might take to pump her out and raise her.

As the evening drew on, Taliaferro's militia, augmented by an angry crowd of civilians, began demonstrating at the navy yard gates, where the untrained recruits of the Third Massachusetts now stood guard. Paulding was acutely aware that the soldiers were raw recruits — they were among the first of Lincoln's seventy-five thousand volunteers — and could not be trusted if the situation deteriorated much further. He could see no other recourse than to put the yard to the torch and destroy everything in it, the *Merrimac* in particular.

Teams of men rowed out to the half-sunken ships and set piles of old cordage, cotton waste, and other burnable matter at critical points, doused the ships with turpentine, and laying off trails of gunpowder and slow match, worked their way from vessel to vessel. Simultaneously, another team, wielding sledgehammers, attempted to destroy the enormous cache of more than one thousand large-caliber guns stored at the yard. The most effective means of destroying a cannon was to knock off one of its trunnions — the stubby cylinders that protruded at right angles from the barrel and that held it in place for firing. But the guns were so well made that after an hour of sweaty hammering, the men managed to destroy only a handful of the older cannon and none of the highly valuable Dahlgrens, the toughest, most reliable weapons in the U.S. Navy's arsenal. The men were reduced to spiking the remaining cannon by driving heavy nails into the priming vents. At best this was only a temporary means of disabling the weapons, since the rebels had only to drill out the spikes to return the guns to service. To make the recovery of the guns as difficult as possible, the Yankees hauled them over to the seawall and threw them into the river.

The most important single facility at the navy yard was its huge granite dry dock, which was large enough to accommodate the biggest ships in the navy and would, if allowed to fall into Southern hands, give the Confederacy the capacity to salvage and construct vessels of any size. To prevent such an event, an officer from the Army Corps of Engineers had accompanied Paulding from Washington with orders to destroy the dock if necessary. Supervising a team of fifty men, he watched as they carefully eased twenty barrels of black powder into the dry dock's hydraulic system and set a train of powder that stopped a safe distance from it.

A little after midnight, with the ships in the yard primed to ignite, every warehouse and barracks packed with explosives and incendiaries, the great dry dock mined and set to explode, and the crowds at the gate and across the river growing ever more menacing and angry, Paulding ordered his men into the ships. A steam tug arrived from Hampton Roads to take the *Merrimac* in tow, but since that was no longer an option, the *Cumberland* was substituted in her place. As the tide turned, Paulding was on the verge of ordering his little squadron downriver when he learned that the disgraced McCauley had decided at the last moment to remain at the doomed navy yard. Cursing the addled old man, Paulding held up the departure long enough to send a detail of men to fetch him. They found him in a disheveled state in his quarters, wild-eyed and utterly confused. They coaxed him to change his mind and accompany them to the waiting *Pawnee*, at which point Paulding gave the order to depart, leaving behind only a handful of men to fire the fuses. In the predawn darkness lit faintly by a half-moon, the *Pawnee* led the little procession of Union ships furtively downstream toward Hampton Roads.

At 4:20 A.M., on an order from the commodore, a rocket from the *Pawnee* signaled the men remaining in the yard to torch the fuses and run for the last boat waiting at the water's edge. All at once, with a series of deep whooshes and thumps, the entire navy yard was ablaze. The officer in charge described how "in a few minutes the whole area of the yard was one sheet of flame — the two ship houses and the whole line of stores, as well as the *Merrimac*."

The conflagration could be seen for thirty miles, a great seething, crackling inferno, a foreshadowing of the terrible war that was to come. Paulding and his staff looked back at the holocaust, taking satisfaction from the fact that even if they had not been able to save the *Merrimac*, they had left little to be salvaged. As they reviewed the plans for their escape — they were still deep in what was now in fact enemy territory — they waited expectantly for the great explosion that would sound the end of the dry dock.

But there was no explosion. Nor was there ever a satisfactory explanation for why the two thousand pounds of black powder failed to ignite.

Perhaps there was a wet fuse or human error of some kind. A rumor has floated around for years that an unidentified Union petty officer deliberately interrupted the powder train to protect the nearby houses of his friends from the granite shrapnel that would have been unleashed by the explosion, but no one has ever been able to authenticate the story. As it was, no one would ever find out for sure why the great dock survived. But they would soon enough learn the awesome price the North would have to pay as a result.

3

"IRON AGAINST WOOD"

When the Virginia militia overran the Norfolk yard the following morning, they discovered that despite the frantic efforts of the escaping Union forces to destroy the base, at least five million dollars' worth of goods and equipment had survived, including hundreds of cannon, crates of small arms, thousands of rounds of ammunition, barrels of gunpowder, and other valuable sea stores. The news was immediately telegraphed to Richmond, along with a listing of the various sunken but recoverable ships captured at the yard. From Richmond the good news was relayed to the capital of the Confederacy, which at that time was in Montgomery, Alabama, where the new secretary of the navy, Stephen Mallory, read it with satisfaction.

Significantly, it was the guns, not the ships, that Mallory viewed as the most valuable prize, particularly the fifty-four new Dahlgrens, the most accurate, most powerful naval guns money could buy. As far as Mallory was concerned, the ships, which for the most part were old and rotting, were not worth pumping out and refitting. Even those that were still sound were built of wood, and Mallory had not the least interest in wooden ships. What he wanted for his tiny navy — what he was already insisting upon — were ironclads.

Mallory, the lone Roman Catholic in Jefferson Davis's inner circle, and therefore somewhat suspect in a largely Anglican and Presbyterian cabinet, is probably one of the most underrated figures in the entire panoply of Civil War leaders. He was a man of daring vision, whose energy and determination were largely responsible for making the Confederate navy an important element in the Southern war effort. He was cut from a very different cloth than his Northern counterpart, Gideon Welles. Where Welles had come into office with little experience in naval matters, and was still striving to master the details of his job, Mallory had spent a lifetime involved with the sea, acquiring a sophisticated understanding of both ships and sailors. As a senator from Florida, he had served as chairman of the Naval Affairs Committee and had a clear grasp of the opportunities and obstacles he faced.

During his years in Washington, Mallory had observed with particular interest the improvements that Britain and France were incorporating into their navies as a result of lessons learned in the Crimean War. The French, particularly, had made great progress in developing armored vessels and had successfully employed ironclad floating batteries to attack the Russian fortress at Kinburn. With the return of peace, the French had launched a highly advanced ironclad in 1859, the oceangoing *Gloire*. She was still essentially a wooden ship, but along the waterline, and up to the gun deck, she was protected by almost five inches of solid armor plate. A nervous Britain responded by constructing an even larger and more powerful ironclad, HMS *Warrior*, which was built entirely of iron. Mallory was determined that the Confederate Navy would include ships as modern, powerful, and impregnable as those of the two European powers.

Early in May 1861, only a fortnight after the fall of the Norfolk yard, he set about making his vision a reality. He wrote to the Confederate House Committee of Naval Affairs: "I regard the possession of an iron-armored ship as a matter of the first necessity." Such a vessel, he contended, could range the entire coast of the United States — which, by his reckoning, stretched only from Maine to Maryland — destroying naval and commercial shipping and laying waste the enemy's seaports. "Should the committee deem it expedient to begin at once the construction of such a ship, not a moment should be lost. Inequality of numbers may be compensated by invulnerability. Not only does economy, but naval success, dictate the wisdom and expediency of fighting with iron against wood, without regard to first cost."

Such grandiose sentiments were all well and good, but where was Stephen Mallory to find such ships? The Confederate economy was almost totally based on agriculture and slave labor, and the industrial capacity of the whole region was less than that of New York City. The South had neither the means nor the ability to forge steel or manufacture machine tools, and could muster neither the facilities nor the skills to create such a complex undertaking as an ironclad steamer. The only way the South could get the ironclads it needed, Mallory argued, was to buy them in Europe. Impressed as much by Mallory's enthusiasm as by his logic, the Confederate congress quickly voted him two million dollars to buy his ironclad navy, and Mallory, with equal alacrity, dispatched Lieutenant James D. Bulloch to Europe the following day, with orders to purchase, or arrange to have built, six ironclad steamers. The secretary was particularly hopeful that Bulloch might be able to buy the *Gloire* herself from the French.

Meanwhile, the hulk of the *Merrimac*, still mired in the ooze of the shallow waters of the Norfolk Navy Yard, was proving to be an annoying obstruction to navigation, and the Confederate officers in charge of getting the yard back into operation ordered her raised, simply to get her out of the way. A team of engineers sealed her bottom and pumped her out, and in due course she once more rose to the surface, a ravaged semblance of her former self, burned down to her berth deck, with neither masts nor rigging. At first glance, she was nothing more than a useless hulk, yet for all the damage she had sustained, she remained a large and formidable vessel, and the sight of her, lying low in the water, must have suggested to at least some observers the possibility of converting her to some useful purpose.

In those early weeks of the war, as both sides frantically positioned themselves for the clash of arms to come, Stephen Mallory was alternatively encouraged and disappointed by the news flowing into Montgomery. He was delighted when Virginia and North Carolina joined the Confederacy — a move that prompted the decision to move the seat of government to Richmond — but he was distressed by the lukewarm response to the war evidenced by the news from Europe. The South had entered the war confident that both Britain and France would rally to its support, if only to ensure a steady supply of cotton for their textile mills, but it quickly became apparent that such confidence was unwarranted. Britain issued a proclamation of neutrality, which recognized the Confederacy as a belligerent, but made no further move to help. And even before Mallory's purchasing agents had a chance to report back on their mission to buy ironclad steamers, he learned from other sources that both Britain and France had become involved in an ironclad building rivalry, which meant that neither power was likely to be able to fill any Confederate orders for such ships. If Mallory wanted ironclads, it seemed, he was going to have to find them somewhere else.

Consequently, on the evening of June 3, 1861, the same day Mallory arrived at the new Confederate capital of Richmond, he met with Lieutenant John Mercer Brooke, an ordnance specialist and one of his most trusted advisers, to consider a new and heretofore unexamined possibility: Could the South build its own ironclads? The two men conferred long into the night. It was a formidable challenge, given the South's woefully meager manufacturing capacity, and Mallory made the prospect all the more daunting by insisting on a *seagoing* ironclad, a ship that could steam north and ravage the Yankee coast.

Brooke understood iron, but he was not a naval architect. Although the two men continued their discussion over a number of days, they failed to come up with a plan to match Mallory's goal. After consulting with engineers at the Tredegar Iron Works in Richmond, Brooke was finally able to put together rough plans for an ironclad vessel that could be constructed locally, and that even gave promise of fulfilling the seagoing capabilities the secretary wanted.

It was, of necessity, a simple design, essentially an armored raft, powered by steam, armed with broadsides of guns, to port and starboard. Mallory quickly approved the sketches, and at the secretary's request, Brooke completed "outline drawings — body, sheer and deck plans" for the proposed ship. On June 23 the two men met with John L. Porter, a naval ship constructor who, like Brooke, was a U.S. Navy veteran who had "gone

South," and William P. Williamson, the Confederate navy's chief engineer. With the details settled, Porter, a trained naval architect, was left to make a fresh set of plans, while Brooke and Williamson went off to find engines and boilers for their proposed vessel. When they were unable to find what they wanted at the Tredegar works, they set off by train the following morning to see what they might come up with at Norfolk.

On their arrival at the navy yard, they made a preliminary search that proved equally futile, until Williamson suggested that they take a look at the engines in the recently raised *Merrimac*, which was now resting on keel blocks in the dry dock. These were the same engines that had been condemned when the ship returned from the Orient, the same ones that Benjamin Isherwood had reassembled and jury-rigged in his frantic efforts to save the *Merrimac* for the U.S. Navy.

In a cursory examination of the machinery, the two men were pleased to discover that the *Merrimac*'s engines had suffered only minor damage as a result of being submerged in the Elizabeth River. Encouraged, the chief engineer, perhaps already prompted by a fresh thought, broadened his inspection to include an examination of the structural elements of the lower portions of the ship. On determining that the hull itself was still sound, he turned to Brooke and made a radical proposal: Why not turn the *Merrimac* into an ironclad? Instead of starting from scratch, they could simply iron-plate the damaged but easily repaired hull that was already in dry dock. It would save hundreds of thousands of dollars and months of effort. The startled Brooke needed only a moment to consider the bold simplicity of the idea and enthusiastically agreed to it.

Williamson's inspiration solved a number of problems, but the idea had some obvious drawbacks as well, not the least of which was the fact that they would have to contend with the *Merrimac*'s very deep draft of twenty-three feet, which would make it impossible for her to operate anywhere near shoal waters. Brooke admitted later, "We all thought the draught too great, but we could not do better." Even if he had any objections at the time, he felt strongly that the idea was simply too good to overlook. He and Williamson hurried back to Richmond, and after explaining their new plan to Porter and convincing him of its feasibility, they outlined it to Mallory, who was excited by the possibility of so quickly getting an ironclad into action and promptly gave his approval. On July 11, 1861, barely a month after his first meeting with Brooke in Richmond, Mallory sent an order to Flag Officer French Forrest, commandant of the Norfolk Navy Yard, to commence work: "You will proceed with all practicable dispatch to make the changes in the *Merrimac*, and to build, equip, and fit her in all respects, according to the designs and plans of the constructor and engineer, Messrs. Porter and Williamson. As time is of the utmost importance in this matter, you will see that the work progresses without delay to completion."

The following day, a warship of unparalleled power and terror began to take shape in the dry dock at the Norfolk Navy Yard.

4

ENTER MR. BUSHNELL

In the same week that Stephen Mallory gave the
order to transform the *Merrimac* into a Confederate ironclad, his Northern counterpart took a
first tentative step toward instituting a similar
modernization of the Union navy. On July 4,
1861, Gideon Welles submitted his first report to
Congress, a lengthy document detailing his efforts to put the navy on a wartime footing. The
report included a list of recommendations for
further legislation, and toward the end of it, almost as an afterthought, he broached a new subject.

"Much attention has been given within the last
few years to the subject of floating batteries, or
iron-clad steamers," he noted, pointing out that
"other governments, and particularly France and
England, have made it a special object in connex-
ion with naval improvements." While those other
governments clearly considered the commission-
ing of ironclad warships a matter of first importance, Welles made it clear that his department
attached no such urgency to the issue, and even
suggested that the present period "is perhaps not

one best adapted to heavy expenditures by way of experiment." He would, however, "recommend the appointment of a proper and competent board to enquire into the matter," so that Congress might, in its wisdom, decide at some future date whether or not to authorize the construction of such a vessel.

If Secretary Welles had hoped that his somewhat diffident rallying cry for ironclads might galvanize the Congress, he soon learned otherwise. The July session was the first meeting of Congress since the start of the war, and the representatives and senators were busy reorganizing both houses, which had been thrown into disarray as a result of the withdrawal of so many members from the seceding states. Whatever time the congressmen had left over from housekeeping chores was spent negotiating for fat new government contracts on behalf of their constituents back home. They had neither interest nor inclination to give much thought to ironclad warships.

The apparently tentative interest in the subject of ironclads on the part of Gideon Welles may be explained by the overwhelming complexity of his principal responsibility, which was the extremely difficult task of mounting a viable blockade of the Confederacy.

Welles had argued strenuously against such a blockade, but Lincoln had demanded it. In those early months of the war, the president relied heavily on General Winfield Scott for advice on military matters. Scott, who had been a hero of the Mexican War, was by that time far too old for field command, but his mind was still keen, and he had advocated, and Lincoln had adopted, the so-called Anaconda Plan, a strategy that would remain the centerpiece of the Union war effort throughout the next four years. The Anaconda Plan called for the Union to encircle the Confederate states, seizing control of the Mississippi as well as the Atlantic and Gulf coasts, and cutting off all access to foreign suppliers, until, like the eponymous South American constrictor, the Union forces were in a position to squeeze the Confederacy into submission. The key element of the Anaconda Plan was the blockade, and the president was determined to mount one, regardless of cost.

Welles pointed out that blockades are tricky things at best, containing all sorts of legal snares and diplomatic complications that require constant attention. The blockade of the South was going to be a particularly ambitious undertaking, because it called for establishing and maintaining an effective naval cordon along the entire length of the Confederacy's complicated coastline, which stretched 3,500 miles from Virginia to the Mexican border. Welles pointed out that the federal navy, with its forty-two mostly obsolescent ships, was totally inadequate to such a project. Besides, the secretary argued, a blockade made a mockery of Lincoln's claim that the war was simply a rebellion: A nation did not blockade its own ports, he pointed out, it closed them. For the

United States to station squadrons off the Southern coast, denying passage to ships entering or leaving, constituted a de facto recognition of the Confederacy as a sovereign power and thereby invited foreign powers to extend diplomatic relations to the South, with potentially disastrous consequences for the Union.

Lincoln listened to the navy secretary's reasoned arguments but overrode all objections. He was determined to have his blockade, and it was therefore up to Gideon Welles to make it a reality. One of the secretary's greatest difficulties arose from the fact that it was generally recognized in the international community that a blockading nation not only must declare its intention to halt trade but must deploy a large enough force to make the threat effective. Anything less than a clear command of the blockaded waters was known as a "paper blockade," and foreign trading vessels were free to ignore it and travel with impunity to and from restricted ports under the full protection of their governments. Such paper blockades, Welles knew, could be far more damaging to the blockading power than no blockade at all, for they would almost certainly incur the wrath of foreign powers, with unforeseen consequences.

In a desperate effort to create, almost overnight, a large enough navy to mount a blockade, Welles sent agents to every seaport in the Union to buy up virtually any vessel that could float and was large enough to carry a gun. The ragtag assortment of tugs, ferryboats, and other harbor craft hurriedly mustered into service became known as "the soapbox navy." It would eventually prove to be surprisingly effective in the shallow waters off the Confederate coast, sealing off Southern ports and strengthening the blockade at a time when Welles despaired of its ever becoming a viable force.

It was the sensitive diplomatic aspects of the blockade that made Welles's job particularly difficult. Everyone involved in the conflict, North and South, recognized that the war was more than just a local quarrel. There was a third party to the argument, namely Europe, and more specifically Britain and France. When the Southern states had opted for war, it was with the openly expressed expectation that the European powers would come to their support, in part because British and French textile mills were dependent upon Southern cotton, and in part because there were obvious advantages to the European powers in splitting the increasingly powerful United States into two or more independent, and therefore weaker, entities. If Britain and France were to manifest such support for the Confederacy, it would vastly increase the South's ability to wage war and would in all likelihood result in a negotiated peace, which almost certainly meant a Southern victory. The European powers had failed as yet to provide the diplomatic recognition the South so assiduously sought, but the possibility that they might do so at any moment was very much at the top of everyone's mind in Washington.

Welles had to contend with a crucial question: Would the blockade intimidate the European powers, causing them to keep their distance, or would it arouse their anger and lead them to tilt toward support for the South? Just how serious that danger could be to the Union cause became evident in the summer of 1861, when Rear Admiral Sir Alexander Milne, commanding a Royal Navy squadron in the Caribbean, declared that if the Union blockade allowed as few as three blockade runners to escape its clutches, he could consider the blockade invalid, and foreign merchant shipping thereafter would be free to trade openly with the Confederate states. The vision of hundreds of European merchantmen crowding into Southern ports, delivering a flood of arms and war goods in exchange for raw cotton, was enough to ruin the sleep of every politician in Washington. Not until Queen Victoria's embarrassed foreign secretary emphatically disavowed Milne's eccentric "three ship" test of a blockade's legitimacy did the men in Lincoln's cabinet rest easy on the matter.

It was, ironically enough, Gideon Welles's immersion in the problems of the blockade, and particularly how the blockade related to Virginia, that forced him to return to the question of ironclad vessels.

The northern anchor of the blockade was the

entrance to Chesapeake Bay, which was bracketed by Cape Charles to the north and Cape Henry to the south. As long as Union forces held that key gateway to the Atlantic, they controlled access to all of Virginia's most important ports. The key to the Chesapeake, in turn, was Hampton Roads. That strategic body of water, just inside the capes and well protected from the nearby Atlantic, had remained in Union hands from the outset of hostilities and was dominated by the Union guns of Fort Monroe augmented by a large squadron of Union warships.

Because of its location and its close proximity to Washington, Hampton Roads was recognized from the start as the most important link in the blockade, and in consequence, all matters relating to Hampton Roads were handled as top priority. So it was that Welles and his staff were instantly brought up short when, only a few days after the secretary had delivered his report to Congress, disturbing rumors began to reach the Navy Department concerning the work commencing on the *Merrimac*. Spies in Richmond and Norfolk soon confirmed the reports, and it quickly became apparent that the rebels at Gosport were turning the erstwhile Union frigate into an ironclad of such proportions that it was impossible for them to keep it secret. The frightening realization of just how dangerous such a vessel would be to the forces guarding Hampton Roads, and therefore to the maintenance of the blockade, brought an entirely new sense of urgency to the question of ironclad warships for the Union navy. Welles, who only a fortnight before had discounted their importance, now found them to be the most urgent matter on his agenda.

The secretary and his staff were suddenly faced with a major crisis. Just how was the United States to combat the threat posed by the resurrected *Merrimac*? The obvious solution was to build an even stronger ironclad than the rebel ship, but how was that to be accomplished, particularly since the Confederates had such a distinct head start? Welles began to cast about for some means of alerting Congress to the peril and persuading it to immediately authorize the Ironclad Board he had so diffidently suggested in his report. Welles had neither the time nor the talent to light a fire under Congress, but he knew a man who had both — and who in the end would have almost as much to do with the creation of the *Monitor* as Ericsson himself.

His name was Cornelius S. Bushnell, a bright, quick-witted venture capitalist from New Haven, a man with a talent for getting things done. Born in poverty, Bushnell had by the age of thirty-one already amassed a personal fortune that made him one of the richest and most influential men in Connecticut. He was active in shipping, wholesaling, and railroads, and it was during his attempt to expand the franchise of his New Haven & New London Railroad that he had learned how to maneuver and manipulate, first lobbying the legislature in Hartford, and later the Congress in Washington.

Welles, in his days as a Hartford newspaper-man, had watched Bushnell in action and been impressed by the younger man's energy and parliamentary skills. Within days of the first reports about the *Merrimac*, the secretary arranged a meeting with Bushnell and confided his anxieties concerning the news of the ironclad under construction in Norfolk. He described the threat such a vessel posed to the Union, and explained his own frustration at his inability to get Congress to do anything about it. Would Bushnell, who knew his way around the corridors of power, agree to help? The fact was not lost on either man that an enterprising person such as Bushnell might find some business coming his way if an ironclad bill were passed. The younger man immediately agreed, and later that evening Gideon Welles showed up at the Willard Hotel, where Bushnell was staying, with a draft of the desired bill. The following morning Bushnell, with Welles's draft in his pocket, set out for Capitol Hill to see if he could make it law.

Welles's faith in Bushnell's persuasive abilities proved well founded. By July 19, Bushnell had arranged for a certain Senator James Grimes of Iowa to introduce Bill 36 establishing the Ironclad Board and authorizing $1.5 million for the construction of ironclad warships. Helped by a flood of continuing rumors and reports about the *Merrimac*, he managed to get the bill through both houses in a matter of days. On August 3, Lincoln signed the bill into law, and Welles, now armed with an authorization to spend money, immediately advertised for bids for ships "either of iron or wood and iron combined for sea or river service to be of not less than ten nor over sixteen feet draught of water." The vessels were to carry between 80 and 120 tons of armor, and to carry provisions for up to three hundred men for sixty days, along with enough coal for eight days of steaming. He appointed a board to examine the proposals for such ships, consisting of Commodores Joseph Smith and Hiram Paulding and Captain Charles H. Davis.

By the first week of September, the board had received sixteen proposals, out of which it selected two. The first was an ambitious seagoing steamer of 4,120 tons submitted by Merrick and Sons of Philadelphia, designed along the lines of the new European ironclads. She would eventually be named the *New Ironsides*. The second selection was a plan proposed, not surprisingly, by Bushnell for a considerably smaller warship of 950 tons that would eventually be christened the *Galena*, in honor of General Ulysses Grant's hometown. In awarding the grant for the second design, the board expressed concern that the ship might not be able to carry the rail and plate armor specified, and stipulated that Bushnell would have to furnish proof of the ship's stability before it granted final approval.

Bushnell was a sharp businessman, but he had no particular knowledge of ship construction, and he was unsure how to get the proof the board requested. He returned to his rooms at the Willard and sought the advice of one of his partners, Cornelius Delamater, proprietor of the Novelty Iron Works of New York. Delamater advised him to consult his friend John Ericsson, a New York engineer with whom he had maintained a close business and personal relationship of many years standing, and who thoroughly understood modern shipbuilding construction. Bushnell thanked him and set off for New York that night. The next morning he called on Ericsson at his home in Manhattan and showed him the questioned plans for his steam-powered ironclad. Ericsson looked at them briefly and asked him to return the following morning for his answer.

As instructed, Bushnell returned on September 19 and was pleased to receive the Swedish engineer's assurances that his ship would be not only stable but capable of withstanding a six-inch shot, provided it was fired "from a respectable distance." With their business concluded, Ericsson asked his visitor if he had time to look at some plans of his own for an impregnable floating battery that could be built in ninety days. The surprised Bushnell was immediately interested and told Ericsson that such a vessel was precisely what the Navy Department was looking for, and that the best his designer had been able to come up with was the ship that the two men had just been discussing.

As Bushnell would tell the story years later,

Ericsson then pulled out a storage box, took from it the plans of his "sub-aquatic system of naval warfare," and showed his visitor the little cardboard model. He described the novel nature of his little warship in detail, and in less than ten minutes convinced an excited Bushnell that his design was precisely what was needed in the emergency. Bushnell implored Ericsson to let him show the plans to his friend Gideon Welles. Ericsson said he was happy to have him do so, but he warned that there was a history of bad blood between himself and the U.S. Navy. He recounted the sorry story of the *Princeton* and warned Bushnell it was highly unlikely that the navy would even consider his design once it knew its origin.

Bushnell was undeterred. He was a convert to Ericsson's little ship and convinced of its importance. He assured the inventor that if the navy proved intransigent, he was sure he could find some means of overcoming its objections. He and Ericsson struck a bargain to work together should the design be accepted, and with Ericsson's blessings Bushnell took the plans and the little model and departed for Hartford, whither Welles had returned home for a few days.

Bushnell was aware that Lincoln had recently grown apprehensive about the possible intervention of England in the war, so when he walked into the Secretary's home the following day, he brandished Ericsson's plans overhead and announced cheerfully that the president "need not further worry about foreign interference; I have discovered the means of perfect protection." (It is not without significance that Gideon Welles's first knowledge of the *Monitor* came in the context of a perceived threat from Britain, not the Confederacy.)

The two men examined the designs, and as Welles listened to Bushnell's excited explication, he began to share the younger man's enthusiasm. He urged Bushnell to hurry back to Washington and get the Ironclad Board to examine and recommend the plan. He would himself return later in the week, and he promised Bushnell a contract to build the ship.

The following evening, a Saturday, Bushnell was again back on the train, this time bound for Washington. On Sunday morning, September 22, after breakfast at the Willard Hotel, he arranged to meet two other business partners who were in town, John F. Winslow and John A. Griswold. Both men were industrialists from Troy, New York, who were subcontractors on Bushnell's own ironclad project. They were intimately familiar with the iron trade and, more important, as it turned out, with the intricacies of New York politics.

The three men were all aware that wartime Washington was a hotbed of spying and intrigue. Southern sympathizers, known as Copperheads, were everywhere, and to ensure that their conversation would remain private, Bushnell hired a carriage, so that they might speak openly during

76

a ride through the Washington suburbs. It was that secret meeting in the carriage, and the events that arose from it, that more than any other single factor secured the eventual success of the *Monitor*. It is likely that without the cunning and string pulling of those three Yankee businessmen, and the scheme they hatched that Sunday afternoon, the navy would never have agreed to build the ship that saved the blockade.

Winslow and Griswold were no more ship-builders than Bushnell, but as they examined the plans and listened to his explanation, they grasped both the exciting prospects of the pro-posed ship and the problems inherent in the navy's animosity toward its designer. Bushnell, with his obvious enthusiasm for the project, and his close relationship with Gideon Welles, was a compelling and influential figure, but the two businessmen from Troy could bring another im-portant element to the table, namely, their long and close relationship with the ex-governor of New York, William Seward, Lincoln's secretary of state. The three men, after analyzing the situ-ation, devised a campaign to thwart the navy's likely objections, and with that object in mind, agreed to make the State Department their first stop on the following day.

The next morning, Secretary Seward, on learn-ing that his old friends Winslow and Griswold wished to meet with him, immediately made time for the three men and listened attentively as Bush-nell, who was by now well rehearsed in extolling the virtues of the little ironclad, once again described the features of Ericsson's design. The secretary of state quickly became an advocate, and while his visitors were still in his office, dashed off a letter of introduction to the president. That same afternoon — it was now Monday, only four days since Bushnell had first seen the plans in Ericsson's office — the three men met with Lincoln in the White House. Once more Bushnell spread out the plans and explained the features of the strange and wonderful craft. Lincoln was taken with the proposal. He remarked that he knew little about boats, except for the flatboats he had skippered in his youth, but since Ericsson's boat was as flat as needs be, he understood the good points from the start. He gave his visitors his support and promised he would meet them the following morning in Commodore Smith's office when they presented the proposal to the Ironclad Board. The president cautioned Bushnell that he had no power with the board, but Bushnell took the warning with a grain of salt. He knew that Lincoln's presence at the meeting the next day would undoubtedly carry weight.

The room the following morning was crowded with naval officers young and old, every one of them aware that the president's presence strongly suggested his support for the little ship. Virtually every one of them opposed it, for no other reason than that it had been devised by John Ericsson. Lincoln sat and listened for nearly an hour, and then, when he was preparing to leave, Commodore Smith turned to him and asked what he thought of the novel ship. Lincoln arose from his chair and said that he thought "a good deal as the western girl did when she stuck her foot in the stocking . . . that there was something in it." Then he smiled, bade the group good morning, and left.

On the basis of the president's comments, the two senior members of the board, Smith and Paulding, were prepared to recommend the proposal if the junior member, Captain Davis, was willing to agree. But Davis was adamant in his opposition and could not be moved. When Bushnell tried one final time to persuade him, the captain turned to him with a smirk and, in a coy reference to the Second Commandment, told him he could gather up his plans and take them home and worship them if he so desired, "as they were not like anything in the heavens above, or the earth beneath, or in the waters under the earth."

It was a morning for quotable sallies.

After all the high hopes and the carefully devised campaign to secure a contract for Ericsson's design, the sudden and decisive rejection by the board threw Bushnell into a state of momentary despair, but by the afternoon he had recovered his normal optimism and decided on one last ploy: He would try to persuade the stiff-necked Ericsson himself to come down to Washington to defend his ship. Ericsson had told Bushnell categorically that he would not go to the Navy Department under any circumstance, but Bushnell was confident he could get the stubborn Swede to change his mind. He had met the inventor only briefly, but he believed he had the measure of the man. By the time his train reached Baltimore, Bushnell had decided to play on Ericsson's vanity, which he suspected was as mercurial as his famous temper. As he would later recall, he spent the rest of the trip planning his strategy, and after a night's rest at the Astor House in New York, he appeared at nine the following morning at the inventor's door. According to Bushnell's account, a nervous but excited Ericsson was waiting for him.

"What is the result?" Ericsson asked eagerly.

"Magnificent!" Bushnell lied.

A suddenly excited Ericsson demanded details.

"Paulding says that your boat would be the thing to punish those Rebels at Charleston," Bushnell reported.

Ericsson beamed with pleasure, and Bushnell continued, "You have a friend in Washington — Commodore Smith. He worships you. He says those plans are worthy of the genius of an Ericsson!"

The inventor's eyes lit up.

Then Bushnell played his last card. "Captain Davis wants a little explanation in detail which I could not give." He made it sound like a trifling matter.

Ericsson could hardly contain himself. "I will

go today!" he announced with finality.

It was perhaps just as well that Bushnell did not accompany Ericsson to Washington, particularly since the first man the Swede ran into at the Navy Department was Captain Davis himself. In all innocence, Ericsson explained that he was in Washington at Bushnell's suggestion to explain the details of his ship.

Davis stared at him incredulously. "What? The little plan Bushnell had here Tuesday? Why, we rejected it in toto!"

Now it was Ericsson's turn to be surprised. "Rejected it? What for?"

"For want of stability," Davis answered succinctly, as if to lay the matter to rest.

"Stability!" roared the outraged Ericsson. "No craft that ever floated was more stable than she would be! That is one of her great merits!"

Davis looked at the Swede with interest. "Prove it, and we will recommend it," he promised.

Ericsson hurried back to his hotel to prepare his proof, but not before he and Davis had arranged to meet with the secretary of the navy and the other two board members in Gideon Welles's office at one o'clock.

At the appointed hour, a confident Ericsson appeared with a set of diagrams he had drawn up specifically to demonstrate his ship's seaworthiness. He took Welles and the three naval officers through a detailed analysis of the factors governing her stability and went on to urge the adoption of the ship both on its merits and the speed with which she could be built. He closed with a fine patriotic peroration suggesting that a negative vote on the proposed vessel might well be considered tantamount to treason. Ericsson did not want for self-confidence.

Welles ignored this last challenge and polled the three board members. This time Davis, either because he was convinced or because he was thoroughly cowed, joined his two colleagues to recommend the contract. Welles turned happily to Ericsson and told him, "Go home and start her immediately and send Bushnell down next week for the formal contract."

It was exactly eight days since the morning in New York when Ericsson had opened his storage chest and first showed Bushnell his plans.

5

AN AERIAL INTERLUDE

On the hot summer day of August 3, 1861, the U.S. Navy's armed transport *Fanny* could be seen chugging slowly across the calm waters of Hampton Roads from the direction of Fort Monroe, towing behind her a large, open-decked barge that carried a decidedly odd-looking cargo: an immense sphere, about twenty feet in diameter, that dwarfed the crewmen on board the barge and was tethered to the deck by restraining ropes made fast to berthing cleats. The strange object was the latest thing in military intelligence, the world's first waterborne observation balloon, already swollen with hydrogen and ready to take to the air. The gas in the great globe shivered and trembled with every thrust of the *Fanny*'s engines and seemed to give the balloon a sense of life, like some enormous captive jellyfish.

As the *Fanny* and her novel tow approached Sewell's Point on the southern side of the Roads, the steamer's captain selected a spot safely beyond the range of the rebel guns on shore and gave the order to drop anchor. When all was secured, a dashing young adventurer named John

La Mountain, carrying a sketch pad and a spy-glass, clambered into the little wicker basket suspended beneath the balloon and gave the command to release the lines that held him to the earth. Moments later, he and his airship began to rise gently and without effort into the sky, and in a matter of minutes La Mountain found himself two thousand feet above the landscape, eerily alone, and free of all earthly restraint save the single thin cable that held him to the barge, now the size of a matchbox, almost half a mile below.

Standing now in the clear air of the upper altitudes, he could hear the shouts of the Confederate soldiers reacting in surprise to his presence. Stretched out below him on all sides lay a spectacular bird's-eye view of tidewater Virginia. Directly beneath his basket stretched the blue waters of Hampton Roads, an anchorage about three miles across and perhaps seven or eight miles long, which separated the Yankee encampments to the north from the Confederate land batteries to the south. To the west, within the Confederate lines, lay the three rivers that converged to form the Roads: the broad James, which led in a northerly direction toward the capital at Richmond; the somewhat smaller Elizabeth, which rose to the south and flowed past Norfolk on its way to the sea; and the still-smaller Nansemond, which flowed in from the west. At the opposite end of the Roads, on the far side of Fort Monroe at Old Point Comfort, lay the great reaches of

Chesapeake Bay, and beyond the Virginia Capes, easily visible from the balloon, the gray-green immensity of the Atlantic Ocean.

Taken together, the various elements of the scene spread out beneath him represented one of the most interesting — and strategically significant — meeting points of land and sea anywhere on earth.

The records imply that La Mountain's primary mission that day was to sketch the gun emplacements under construction at Sewell's Point, and to observe any other Confederate activities from his lofty platform. However, the date of his ascension, which coincides with Lincoln's signing of the Ironclad Board bill, suggests that at least one other objective that day would have been to search for any confirmation of the reports about the reconstruction of the *Merrimac*, thirteen miles south at the Norfolk Navy Yard in Gosport. If La Mountain did in fact discern any such activity there, his notes have not survived. It is likely that the great distance and the normal haze of late summer would have obscured his view and protected the Confederacy's secret. For all that, it would have been obvious to a trained observer like La Mountain that something important was going on in the Norfolk area. The number of Confederate gun emplacements being thrown up along the banks of the Elizabeth, as well as on Craney Island and at Pig Point, indicated that the rebels were going to a great deal of trouble to protect whatever it was they were working on upriver.

A glance to the north would confirm that the Southerners were not the only ones interested in strengthening their positions. The Union army had been equally energetic in the deployment of guns on its side of the Roads. General Benjamin F. Butler had broadened his hold on the tip of the peninsula by occupying and fortifying Newport News Point at the mouth of the James, and reinforced another Yankee gun emplacement at the Rip-Raps — a rocky ledge at the center of the seaway opposite Old Point Comfort. Although it was not evident to the naked eye, it was generally known that the army had also upgraded the size and number of cannon in Fort Monroe's battery. The U.S. Navy was also very much in evidence in the Roads, with a number of warships anchored in the lee of the fort, on watch for blockade runners.

Both sides were clearly intent upon protecting their positions with a maximum show of force.

The reason for all the weaponry lay to the east, within clear sight of the balloonist — the ten-mile stretch of water between Capes Charles and Henry where the Chesapeake gave onto the Atlantic Ocean. It was this doorway to the munitions factories of Europe that the Union was determined to nail shut, and that the Confederacy was equally determined to force open. Its significance could not be overstated. Control of the

Chesapeake Straits was the single most important priority of the entire Union blockade, because it carried with it control of the Chesapeake itself, and the great rivers that led into the coastal plain of Virginia and the very heart of the Confederacy.

Whoever held Hampton Roads held the means of winning the war. It was that simple. For all the heroism of the soldiers on both sides, for all the zeal and attention given to the recruitment and deployment of armies, for all the battlefields that would run red with blood in what would be the most murderous conflict in American history, the fact remained that the Confederacy, which had virtually no industry and no means of manufacturing the tools of war, was almost entirely dependent on European sources for its arms and other military supplies. Without European arms, the South would not be able to mount an effective campaign against the armies of the North, and therefore the war was not going to be decided primarily by land engagements but by the effectiveness of the blockade. It was for that reason that the two fiercely determined antagonists were preparing to commit enormous resources in men, money, and machinery to determine control of a patch of brackish water no more than twenty-four square miles in extent.

Two thousand feet over Sewell's Point, John La Mountain, whose observational duties represented only a tiny fraction of his country's commitment to hold on to Hampton Roads, completed his sketches of the rebel fortifications and signaled the balloon handlers on the raft below to return him to the earth.

6

CONTRACTS, SUBCONTRACTS, AND AN UNWELCOME SURPRISE

John Ericsson was in a state of intense concentration as he made his triumphant return to New York. He was acutely aware that the casting, forging, manufacturing, and assembling of his new ship was likely to be the single greatest challenge ever faced by American industry, and that the ninety-day delivery date Gideon Welles had insisted upon, and to which he had so blithely agreed, left absolutely no room for delay. His sharp mind was already processing a myriad of details, plans, anxieties, and anticipations. Because of the extremely tight schedule, and the hundreds of entirely new elements that would have to be created for the vessel, much of the manufacturing would have to be subcontracted out to specialists. Every one of the parts, from the turret to the anchor, and right down to the rivets and flywheels, each one specially designed and untested, would of necessity have to be assembled at the last minute, with little leeway for modification or adjustment.

It was going to take a considerable amount of seed money to get the enterprise moving, and as soon as he arrived in New York, Ericsson called together a hurried meeting with Bushnell, Griswold, and Winslow and outlined the situation. Thanks to the telegraph, the three men were already aware of Ericsson's success and quickly agreed to form a company with him. Each of the new partners put up ten thousand dollars in return for a quarter interest in the enterprise and an equal share in any subsequent Ericsson ironclads the government might purchase.

On September 27, 1861, the four signed a contract committing themselves to the project and organized a division of labor. Ericsson would be in charge of all the plans and would supervise the actual construction of the vessel. Griswold would be in charge of the intricate finances involved in such a complicated enterprise, and Winslow would find the iron and the all-important armor plate. Bushnell, who had been so instrumental in pushing the project, first through Congress and then through the Ironclad Board, had the fewest responsibilities, in part because he had already contributed so much, and in part because he would be busy supervising the construction of his other ironclad at Mystic Bridge, Connecticut.

In lining up subcontractors, virtually all the major orders went to companies in which the partners already had holdings. The Albany Iron Works, co-owned by Winslow, would furnish some of the armor plating as well as the angle iron for the ship's frame. The Rensselaer Iron Works of Troy, in which Griswold was a partner, would make some of the rivets and the bar iron for the pilothouse. One reason for such sweetheart contracts was the opportunity to pick up additional profits, but there were other, equally practical considerations. With such a complicated project and such a tight schedule, it made sense to rely on suppliers the partners were familiar with, and on whom they could depend.

Almost all the companies involved in the construction of Ericsson's ironclad were in New York State. The one significant exception was H. Abbott and Sons, of Baltimore, which would provide most of the iron plate for the turret. Abbott's rolling mills were the largest and best equipped in the country. The mill used to roll plate for the *Monitor* included three heating and two puddling furnaces, a Nasmyth steam hammer, and a pair of ten-foot rolls. Between them, Abbott and Winslow's Albany works manufactured all the armor plate used in the *Monitor*, the first such plate ever rolled in the United States.

Every aspect of the work involved a compromise between visionary concepts and practical considerations. When Ericsson specified that the turret was to be built of two layers of four-inch iron plate, Abbott told him it would take two months to modify their machinery to turn out such a product, and Ericsson immediately settled for eight layers of one-inch plate.

The actual construction of the ship itself was contracted out to the Continental Iron Works of Greenpoint, in Brooklyn. The Novelty Iron Works of New York City, located on the East River across from Continental, was given the important contract to build the ship's turret, in large part because it was the only firm in the city with the powerful steam-operated presses required to bend heavy iron plates.

There was never any question who would be the major contractor for the ship's machinery. Cornelius Delamater was Ericsson's closest and most trusted friend, and a business partner of long standing. His Delamater Iron Works, located next door to his Novelty Works, would build the main engines, boilers, shafts, and pumps, and the special four-blade propeller Ericsson had designed for the vessel, which everyone was beginning to refer to as the *Ericsson*.

Clute Brothers Foundry, in Schenectady, was selected to build the auxiliary steam engines, along with the gun carriages, the special anchor hoisting mechanism, and the engine room grates.

The consortium worked quickly and with impressive efficiency. As Ericsson would later proudly boast, even as the Navy Department clerks wrote up the contract for his new ship, the iron for the keel plate was being drawn through the rolling mill.

The ship they were so feverishly preparing to build was not precisely the vessel that John Ericsson had proposed to the emperor of France in 1854. In the process of negotiating with the Ironclad Board, Ericsson's design had undergone a sea change, and what remained after the modifications could be more accurately described as a close cousin of the original. Many of the most remarkable features of the 1854 version had been discarded in the name of practicality and speed of manufacture. The mighty steam gun, one of Ericsson's most engaging innovations, had been replaced by a more practical substitute: a pair of huge smoothbore Dahlgren guns, designed by, and cast under the direction of, the navy. The new battery would be one of the very few standardized items in the entire ship. Ericsson's prototorpedoes, or "hydrostatic javelins," designed to bedevil the enemy underwater, were simply discarded.

Also gone was the hemispheric turret, replaced by a simpler, easier-to-build cylindrical turret, which now held two guns rather than the previous single piece. The sloping deck, which would have been difficult to construct, was changed to an equally unconventional but simpler flat design. For all the concessions to simplification, the *Ericsson* remained a dazzlingly original configuration of ideas and innovations.

The hull, which was to be built of three-eighths-inch iron plate, was modest in size for a major warship of the period, just 124 feet long and only six and a half feet deep, which was only half the length of the steam frigate of the day and barely one-third the draft. Mounted directly on top of the hull was what was referred to as the "upper hull," or "raft." This was actually a deck, 172 feet long and forty-one feet across, extending twenty-five feet beyond the bow and stern of the lower hull, and a little more than three feet on either side. It was built of solid oak beams, ten inches square, covered with eight inches of wooden planking, which was in turn covered by two one-inch layers of iron plate. An iron skirt, something like the overhang of a tablecloth, was attached all around the edge and extended down five feet, well below the waterline. Since the ship was designed for a ten-foot draft, the deck would ride only a little over a foot above the surface of the water. The iron skirt would serve to protect the propeller, the rudder, and the hull itself. A cannonball fired at the lower hull would have to pass through twenty-five feet of water to reach it, and since no cannonball on earth could travel through that much water and retain enough velocity to damage the hull, Ericsson felt it was safe to build it of plate only three-eighths of an inch thick.

In the middle of the deck sat the ship's most prominent element, her massive turret, which measured nine feet high and a little over twenty feet in diameter. Its shot-proof walls were built of eight layers of one-inch plate, bolted together with overlapping joints, and lined inside with an additional layer of iron, making the wall nine inches thick overall. The turret weighed 120 tons, even without the guns, and was supported on a brass ring set into the deck. The turret was pierced with two portholes, each one just large enough to admit the muzzle of one of the Dahlgrens. When the guns were withdrawn, the ports could be sealed with huge iron shutters. The roof of the turret was built of solid iron beams and covered over with perforated iron plate, making it shell-proof while at the same time admitting enough daylight for the gun crews to see what they were doing, and allowing for the necessary circulation of air.

In action, when it was necessary for the turret to turn, it was jacked up by a screw-and-wedge mechanism, and the entire weight was taken by a single vertical iron shaft set in the center of the floor. The turret itself was made to revolve by two single-piston donkey engines controlled by a clutch mechanism within the turret.

It was only after construction was under way that the partners learned from a casual comment dropped by Ericsson that a certain Theodore R. Timby, of New York, had tried to interest the War Department in a revolving turret in 1841 and had subsequently applied for a caveat on it in 1843. The partners were immediately concerned that Timby, who was still very much alive, might contest their right to use a similar device. To protect themselves against any such claim, they proposed to pay Timby a royalty of five thousand dollars for the ironclad currently under construction, and another five thousand for any future turreted ironclads they might build. Ericsson protested, claiming that the design of such turning turrets went back to ancient times and could not be patented, but the partners insisted. Eventually Ericsson came to understand the business sense behind such payments and reluctantly agreed to them. Proud as he was, though, he never acknowledged Timby as the inventor of the revolving turret.[*]

The enormous weight of the turret, and the problems inherent in keeping it stable as it turned on its spindle and took the shock of its own guns' recoil and the battering of enemy fire, meant that the underpinnings of the turret had to be particularly solid. Ericsson provided the necessary strength with an extremely heavy central bulkhead that ran across the width of the lower hull directly under the turret. This central bulkhead not only served to support the turret but was also a structural wall that divided the ship in half. The forward section was given over to the officers and men, and the rear section was designed to accommodate the engineering spaces in which were located the boilers, main engine, auxiliary machinery, pumps, and coal bunkers.

[*] Ultimately, in July 1862, Theodore Timby converted his caveat into a full patent, defined as an "improvement in revolving battery-tower."

While Ericsson and his partners were busy putting together the network of suppliers required to create an entirely new kind of ship in an impossibly brief time span, the navy, in its collective wisdom, was busy marshaling its most senior officers in a last-ditch attempt to scuttle the project. Many in the navy's old guard were outraged that the Ironclad Board had accepted the design of the mistrusted and despised Ericsson, and they made little attempt to hide their anger. Even Gideon Welles, as he would later record, found himself the object of "obloquy and ridicule" for his stand in favor of the Ericsson ironclad. If the ship were to prove a failure, Welles knew the navy would never let him survive in office. To protect himself against such a potential disaster, he allowed his staff to put together a remarkably mean-spirited contract for the ship, a business document that was totally out of keeping with the enthusiastic support he had shown Ericsson only a few days before.

A week after the agreement was struck, Cornelius Bushnell returned to the Navy Department, as Welles had requested, to pick up the contract. As he read it over for the first time, he was shocked by the stringent conditions the navy had decided to attach to the agreement. Close as the ties were between Welles and Bushnell, the harsh terms and arbitrary nature of the document must have strained their friendship severely.

It began innocently enough.

"This Contract, in two parts, made and entered into this Fourth day of October, Anno Domini, One Thousand Eight Hundred and Sixty-one, between J. Ericsson of the City of New York, as principal, and John F. Winslow, John A. Griswold and C.S. Bushnell, as sureties on the first part, and Gideon Welles, Secretary of the Navy, for and in behalf of the United States on the second part, Witnesseth: —"

The second paragraph held the first surprise. It began with a formal definition of the proposed vessel that was unexceptional. "That in consideration of the payments hereinafter provided for, the party of the first part hereby contracts and agrees to construct an Iron-Clad Shot-Proof Steam Battery of iron and wood combined on Ericsson's plan; the lower vessel to be wholly of iron, and the upper vessel of wood; the length to be one hundred and seventy-nine (179) feet, extreme breadth 41 feet and depth five feet, or larger, if the party of the first part should think it necessary to carry the armament and stores required. The vessel to be constructed of the best materials and workmanship throughout, according to the plan and specifications hereto annexed forming a part of this contract."

Then, about halfway through the paragraph, the navy revealed its first surprise. "In addition to said specifications the party of the first part hereby agrees to furnish masts, spars, sails and rigging of sufficient dimensions to drive the vessel at the rate of Six Knots per hour in a fair breeze of wind." Bushnell was nonplussed. There had never been any talk of a sailing vessel. She was to be powered by steam alone, and all parties had understood that fact. Not only would masts and rigging be ineffective, they would totally defeat the single most important design feature in the ship: the ability of the turret to traverse and fire in any direction. Clearly, this mischievous new requirement was designed solely to provide the navy brass with a deal breaker, an excuse to renege on their agreement should they choose to do so.

The closing portion of the paragraph was as unexceptional as the opening. "And the said party of the first part will also furnish in addition to the said specifications a Condenser for making fresh water for the boilers on the most approved plan. And the party of the first part further contracts and engages that the said vessel shall have proper accommodations for her stores of all kinds, including provisions for one hundred persons for ninety days, and shall carry 2500 gallons of water in tanks; that the vessel shall have a speed of Eight sea miles or knots per miles under steam for twelve consecutive hours, and carry fuel for her engines for eight days' consumption at that speed, the deck of the vessel when loaded to be Eighteen inches above load line amidships; that she shall possess sufficient stability with her armament, stores, and crew on board for safe sea-service in traversing the Coast of the United States; that her crew shall be properly accommodated, and that the apparatus for working the Battery shall prove successful and safe for the purpose intended, and that the vessel, machinery and appointments in all their parts shall work to the entire satisfaction of the party of the second part."

The next paragraph spelled out the finances, and it, too, provided some unwelcome surprises. "And the party of the second part agrees to pay for the vessel completed as aforesaid after trial and satisfactory test the sum of Two hundred and seventy-five thousand dollars in coin or Treasury notes at the option of the party of the second part in the following manner, to wit — When the work shall have progressed to the amount of Fifty thousand dollars in the estimation of the Superintendent of the vessel on the part of the United States, that sum shall be paid to the party of the first part on certificate of said Superintendent, and thereafter similar payments according to the certificates of said Superintendent, deducting, reserving and retaining from each and every payment, Twenty-five percentum, which reservation shall be retained until after the completion and satisfactory trial of the vessel, not to exceed ninety days after she shall be ready for sea."

In other words, the government was to hold back a full quarter of the payment for up to three months after delivery of the ship. In addition, the navy had reserved an even more stringent condition for the next paragraph. "And it is further agreed between the said parties that the said vessel shall be completed in all her parts and appointments for service, and any omission in these specifications shall be supplied to make her thus complete; and in case the said vessel shall fail in performance for speed for sea-service as before stated, or in the security or successful working of the turret and guns with safety of the vessel and the men in the turret, or in her buoyancy to float and carry her Battery as aforesaid, then, and in that case, the party of the first part hereby bind themselves, their heirs, executors, administrators and assigns, by these presents, to refund to the United States the amount of money advanced to them on said vessel within thirty days after such failure shall have been declared by the party of the second part, and the party of the first part acknowledge themselves indebted to the United States in liquidated damages to the full amount of money advanced as aforesaid."

Ericsson and his partners were forced to take the entire risk upon themselves. If the ship failed in any way — and it was up to the Navy to decide what constituted failure — the company would be required to provide a money-back guarantee.

"And it is further agreed that the vessel shall be held by the United States as collateral security until said amount of money advanced as aforesaid shall be refunded."

The penultimate paragraph was a standard escape clause protecting the government against the evils and political influence: "And the party of the first part does further engage and contract that no member of Congress, officer of the navy, or any person holding any office or appointment under the Navy Department, shall be admitted to any share or part of this contract or agreement, or to any benefit to arise thereupon."

The wholesale political corruption involved in the letting of military contracts, which would reach scandalous proportions as the war continued, was already evident in the early months of the conflict. Legal restrictions such as the one written into the contract with John Ericsson were an attempt to limit the practice, but it was so pervasive that everyone accepted it as a regrettable but necessary cost of doing business with the government. No one was entirely free of its taint. It was something of an open secret in government circles that Representative Erastus Corning, a member of Congress from upstate New York, was a partner of Winslow's in the Albany Iron Works and therefore stood to profit from the construction of Ericsson's ship. In all likelihood it had been Corning's wire pulling that had made it possible for Bushnell to move the ironclad bill through Congress so expeditiously, after Gideon Welles had failed.

"And it is hereby expressly provided, and this contract is upon express condition, that if any such member of Congress, officer of the navy, or persons above named shall be admitted to any share or part of this contract, or any benefit to arise under it, or in case the party of the first part shall in any respect fail to perform this contract on their part, the same may be at the option of the United States, declared null and void, without affecting their rights to recover for defaults which may have occurred."

Congressman Corning, please note.

In closing, the contract offered a small lagniappe. "It is further agreed between the said parties that such vessel and equipments in all respects shall be completed and ready for sea in one hundred days from the date of this indenture."

In exchange for what can only be characterized as a mean-spirited and unwarranted breach of faith, the navy was willing to give the consortium an extra ten days to deliver the ship.

7

"ERICSSON'S FOLLY"

The onerous provisions inserted into the Ericsson contract came close to scuttling the *Monitor* project. Many years later, when the war was safely won, Cornelius Bushnell attempted to make light of the contract's burdensome conditions, implying that such severe measures as the enforced money-back guarantee and the withholding of 25 percent of the fees were standard provisions in government contracts of the period, mere formalities that were not to be taken literally. But the facts belie him. The pusillanimous penalties incorporated into the *Monitor* contract were in fact highly unusual, and the men who were asked to sign the document understood that clearly. Ericsson was willing to sign because he had been waiting half a lifetime for the opportunity to build his ship, and Bushnell would sign because he trusted Gideon Welles. But Griswold and Winslow refused outright and were prepared to see the enterprise founder before they would tie themselves up in such an arbitrary and one-sided legal agreement.

The situation was aggravated when the navy

announced that it had selected Chief Engineer Alban C. Stimers to serve as the supervisor of the project, the on-site representative who would ensure that the ship met specifications. Stimers was young, smart, and arrogant, with a reputation for being coarse, overbearing, and disagreeable. It was quite enough that the partners had to endure Ericsson's short temper and imperious egoism. Would they have to deal with an equally rude and untrusting naval officer as well? As it turned out, Stimers and Ericsson quickly discovered they were soul mates, with almost identical views on engineering matters, and got along famously from the start.

Perhaps encouraged by that unexpected turn of events, Winslow and Griswold were at last persuaded to take the gamble, and as soon as they signed on, the project roared ahead at full throttle. On October 25, the same day that Ericsson signed with his subcontractors, the ship's keel was laid at the Continental Iron Works, and the construction of the ship was under way.

The creation of the *Monitor* was a flexing of American industrial muscle that is still impressive to contemplate. No single aspect of the Civil War more clearly defines the enormous industrial superiority of the North over the South than a comparison of the means by which each side went about the business of building the two ironclads that would eventually confront one another at Hampton Roads.

In both cases the project was given the highest priority, but as the Confederate team working in Norfolk was to discover time and gain, sometimes all the intelligent planning, determination, and brave inspiration in the world are not enough. There is a sense of agonizing frustration that hangs over the story of the ironcladding of the *Merrimac*, making it a saga of unending effort, a struggle against virtually insurmountable odds.

The availability of iron throughout the South was problematic at best, and the constructor at the Norfolk yard could depend on only one supplier, the Tredegar works in Richmond. Even that source could not be relied upon with any degree of certainty. Some three hundred tons of scrap iron from the burned portions of the Norfolk yard were shipped to Tredegar to be reworked for use in the *Merrimac*, but everyone knew the job would require far more than that. To augment the trickle of iron they were able to come up with from other sources, the Confederates were forced to scavenge railroad iron from captured Chesapeake and Ohio lines, and dig up unused trolley tracks. Even when Tredegar managed to find ample supplies for its rolling mills, getting the finished goods to Norfolk became a major problem. At one point a hundred tons of iron plate lay on the sidings at Richmond for four weeks awaiting a train to get it to the navy yard. In a move to conserve equipment and fuel, the government in Richmond issued an order limiting trains to a top speed of no more than ten miles per hour. Despite such precautions, there were so many disruptions of service that at one point the delivery of iron plate to Norfolk had to be routed through Weldon, North Carolina.

Meanwhile, on both sides of the East River in New York, John Ericsson could call upon an almost limitless variety of specialty iron works for his needs, and work on the Union ironclad continued around the clock. At the Delamater works in Manhattan, construction moved ahead on the equipment that would drive the vessel. There were to be two Martin boilers to power the pair of vibrating lever engines designed by Ericsson and geared to turn the same drive shaft simultaneously. These were formidable engines, with pistons three feet in diameter, that could turn out 320 horsepower and were calculated to move the ship through the water at nine knots. The same firm was also busy casting the specially designed four-bladed propeller, nine feet in diameter, that was to drive the vessel.

Next door, at the Novelty Iron Works, construction began on the great turret. Most of the iron plate required for the project was shipped north from the Abbott Company in Baltimore, which had the biggest rolling mills in the country and was the only firm capable of filling such a large order. (One of the most intriguing "what-ifs" relating to the construction of the *Monitor* concerns the central role played by the Abbott Company. If the state of Maryland had joined the

Confederacy after Fort Sumter, as many expected, Abbott's rolling mills would not have been available for Ericsson's project and would instead have been at the disposal of the team working on the *Merrimac*.)

The interior diameter of the turret was not quite twenty feet, which made for close quarters when the guns and their crews were in place. When the turret was completed, the workers at Novelty installed the massive port stoppers that had arrived from the Delancey works in Buffalo. The stoppers were huge wrought-iron shields designed to drop down over the portholes when the guns were pulled back into the turret, but Ericsson discovered to his distress that due to an error on his part, only one stopper could be raised at a time, and therefore only one gun fired at a time, effectively cutting the ship's broadside in half. A hurried modification did much to solve the problem, but in practice the stoppers, while they did the job they were designed to do, proved cumbersome and difficult to operate.

The turret now weighed close to its full 120 tons and was far too heavy to be hoisted onto a barge in one piece and shipped across the river to Brooklyn for installation on the ship now nearing completion there. It was therefore painstakingly disassembled, each piece carefully tagged and coded, and the separate elements loaded on barges for the short trip to the Continental works.

By early December, as the construction entered

its final phase and Ericsson's vision was finally translated from flat, scaled-down drawings into full-sized, three-dimensional reality, it was at last possible to fully appreciate the daring and originality of his ideas.

The lower hull, begun on October 25, had long since been completed, and the oversized deck installed upon it. The interior of the vessel was divided into almost precisely equal halves by the huge bulkhead that supported the turret. Virtually all of the rear section was given over to engineering spaces, with the exception of a small area occupied by the galley. The two Martin boilers had already been installed in the most forward position, up against the turret's bulkhead. Just behind them, Ericsson positioned the two synchronized engines. Along either side of the boiler and engine rooms ran coal bunkers designed to hold one hundred tons of anthracite, which he calculated would be enough for eight days of steaming. The large-capacity Worthington and Adams pumps, the bilge injection pump, and the rest of the auxiliary machinery were located to the rear. Steam from the boilers was supplied to radiators to create a heating system and to operate the turret. The remaining space was taken up by the propeller shaft and the steering mechanisms connected to the rudder.

Forward of the turret bulkhead lay the half of the ship given over to the crew. At the most forward point of the ship, built into the bow, was Ericsson's unique anchor well, which included a specially designed windlass that allowed crewmen to raise and lower the anchor from inside the ship, so that they were protected from weather and enemy fire. Directly behind the anchor well was the nerve center of the ship, the pilothouse, where the commanding officer, the pilot, and the helmsman were to be stationed. It was a cramped space, a small, heavily armored lookout post that stood about four feet above the level of the deck. It was the ship's principal window on the world. By standing on a ladder and peering through a five-eighths-inch horizontal slot that ran the circumference of the pilothouse, the captain had a full view of surrounding waters. A speaking tube connected the pilothouse to both the turret and the engine room.

The captain's cabin was located behind the pilothouse on the starboard side, and his salon, where he could entertain visitors and carry on the business of the ship, on the port side. In keeping with Ericsson's penchant for elegance and his flare for style, both quarters were fitted out with luxurious appointments and decorated in the highest fashion, with carved rosewood paneling, mohair cushions, and other elegant features. Since all accommodations were below sea level, there were no windows or ports, but Ericsson insisted on draperies throughout the officers' quarters. The captain's cabin contained a private washbasin and head facilities.

This last item provides another example of Ericsson's ability to find practical solutions to difficult problems. His ship was the first ever built in which the entire crew was expected to spend long periods of time, up to a week or more, under water, which created the problem of how to dispose of the crew's waste. Traditionally, ship designers relied on the law of gravity to deal with the problem, constructing places of easement out over the water, usually at the bow, or head, of the ship, so that the waste could fall directly into the sea. But the law of gravity would not suffice when the living quarters were beneath the surface. Ericsson solved the problem with a waste tube that ran from a commode inside the ship to a port in the lower hull that opened to the sea. When waste was introduced into the tube, the interior end could be sealed and the lower end opened, and a pump discharged the contents into the sea. Essentially the same system for evacuating waste was still in use in submarines during the Second World War.

To the rear of the captain's cabin, the officers' staterooms were ranged on either side of the wardroom and fitted out in much the same degree of luxury as that of the captain. While the six-by-eight-foot private cabins were snug, the wardroom itself was surprisingly commodious and allowed for such luxuries as full-length draperies and comfortable furniture.

Aft of the wardroom was the berth deck for the crew, a considerably more Spartan design fitted out with overhead hooks for the sailors' hammocks. To save space, Ericsson provided hooks for only half the crew, since at any given time the other half would be on duty. Storerooms, including the powder magazine and the shell room, bordered the berth deck and filled the remaining spaces of the ship.

Throughout the vessel, illumination was primarily by oil lamps, augmented by disks of heavy glass set into the overhead to provide some modicum of sunlight during the daylight hours.

Soon after New Year's Day, 1862, as preparations were under way for the launching of the new ship, Gustavus V. Fox, the assistant secretary of the navy, wrote Ericsson, asking if he would care to suggest a name for his vessel. On January 20, 1862, the inventor gave him his answer.

Sir:

In accordance with your request, I now submit for your approbation a name for the floating battery at Green Point. The impregnable and aggressive character of this structure will admonish the leaders of the Southern Rebellion that the batteries on the banks of their rivers will no longer present barriers to the entrance of the Union forces.

The iron-clad intruder will thus prove a severe monitor to those leaders. But there are other leaders who will also be startled and admonished by the booming of the guns from the impregnable iron turret. "Downing Street" will hardly view with indifference this last "Yankee notion," this monitor. To the Lords of the Admiralty the new craft will be a monitor suggesting doubts as to the propriety of completing those four steel-clad ships [these were ironclad frigates then under construction by the British] at three-and-a-half millions apiece. On these and many similar grounds I propose to name the new battery Monitor.

Your obedient servant,
J. Ericsson

And so at last, the *Monitor* had a name.

The New York newspapers had closely followed the construction of the new ship, reporting regularly on her progress as she took shape in Brooklyn. Most reporters were highly skeptical of her practicality, and inevitably, some of them had labeled her "Ericsson's Folly." A number of people publicly predicted that she would sink to the bottom of the East River upon launching. It was not only amateurs who distrusted the *Monitor*. Some of the most experienced engineers in the navy were convinced she would sink, and were so sure of their opinions they were willing to put their predictions on the record. The *Monitor* was called an "iron coffin," and on January 30, the date set for her launching, large crowds assembled at the riverside, many of them clearly expecting to witness a disaster. The head of the Continental works, Thomas Rowland, who had supervised the entire construction, was not convinced of the little ship's stability, and just to be on the safe side, quietly arranged for the installation of large wooden airtight tanks under the ship's stern to help ensure her buoyancy.

Ericsson openly scoffed at the doubters and defiantly, in full view of the crowd, took his place on the deck of the new ship, looking out scornfully at the small craft that had been stationed near the launching site, ready to pull survivors from the icy waters should the predicted disaster take place.

At a signal from the inventor, the chocks were pulled from the ways, and the strange-looking craft was allowed to slide into the East River, where to almost everyone's amazement she not only floated but settled easily into the current, riding within three inches of her predicted waterline.

Apparently no one bothered to notice, either then or later, that she carried neither masts, nor rigging, nor sails, as the contract had stipulated. John Ericsson, in his own imperious style, had simply chosen to ignore the requirement.

8

THE RACE FOR
HAMPTON ROADS

A few days prior to the launching of the *Monitor*, Commodore Smith, the senior member of the Ironclad Board, dashed off a brief private letter to Lieutenant John Lorimer Worden, informing him that "I have only time to say I have named you for the command of the battery under contract with Captain Ericsson, now nearly ready at New York. I believe you are the right sort of officer to put in command of her."*

The assignment was no great plum for Worden. So many people in the navy mistrusted Ericsson and disliked his ship that the command might even be seen as a demotion of sorts, although neither Smith nor Worden saw it as such.

Worden was a New Yorker who had served in the navy since his appointment as a midshipman in 1834. He was a slight, sparely built man, soft-

* Ericsson had resigned his commision in the Swedish army in 1827 but continued to use his rank as an honorific.

spoken, but with the soul of a fighting man. One of the officers who would serve under him on the *Monitor*, William F. Keeler, thought him somewhat effeminate in appearance. "Never was a lady the possessor of a smaller or more delicate hand," he wrote to his wife. But Keeler recognized the warrior in his captain, as well. "If I am not very much mistaken, he will not hesitate to submit our iron sides to as severe a test as the most warlike could desire."

Worden had only recently been released from a Southern prison. In the weeks leading up to the war, he had carried secret messages to the beleaguered Union forces occupying Fort Pickens, in Pensacola, Florida. On his way back from that assignment, he was arrested by Confederate authorities and held in prison for seven months, during which his health deteriorated. After his release in November 1861, he returned to the North and was hospitalized to recover from his ordeal. When Smith's letter arrived, he was still considered too weak to return to duty, but ignoring the entreaties of his family and the advice of his doctors, he immediately hurried over to Greenpoint to examine his proposed command. He was impressed by what he saw, and immediately sat down and answered Smith's letter, eagerly accepting the command and requesting that the orders be made official as soon as possible. Only a day or so later, on January 16, he reported for active duty.

In Washington, Gideon Welles continued to worry about the *Merrimac*. In the months since the first rumors of her reconstruction reached Washington, the threat that she posed to the Union war effort had grown ever more tangible. By the middle of October 1861, the navy was receiving regular, reliable reports on the progress of the conversion, and just before Christmas word reached Washington that the Confederates planned to complete her and get her into action by February 1, 1862, well ahead of any possible date for the *Monitor* to make her way down to Hampton Roads to stop her.

Like a queen on a chessboard, the unseen *Merrimac*, even as she stood immobilized in a dry dock far up the Elizabeth River, was exerting enormous influence over Union interests. Perhaps the most noteworthy example of the *Merrimac*'s power to intimidate concerned General George McClellan's ambitious plan for mounting a huge combined services operation to invade the Virginia peninsula between the York and James Rivers, and to drive north and capture Richmond before the rebels had a chance to fortify the city. The highly secret plan called for transporting an army of one hundred thousand troops by sea from Washington to Hampton Roads, disembarking the soldiers at Fort Monroe and Newport News, and heading inland, supported by navy units moving up the James.

While the plan was generally perceived to be

both practical and effective, and promised to shorten the war dramatically, the mere presence of the *Merrimac* at Norfolk threatened to scuttle the entire ambitious scheme. In one of the more bizarre coincidences of the entire Civil War, it so happened that General McClellan had been an official U.S. Army observer in the Crimean War, where he had witnessed the bombardment of Kinburn in 1855, an action in which three French ironclad batteries had destroyed a powerful Russian fort. McClellan had been so impressed by the invincibility of the French ironclads that even the possibility that the *Merrimac* might appear in Hampton Roads to threaten his army caused him to become overcautious, and to postpone his attack and otherwise alter his plans. The *Merrimac*, which had originally been designed to threaten the U.S. Navy's blockade, was now threatening the U.S. Army as well.

While Washington was growing increasingly nervous about the threat of the *Merrimac*, the leaders in Richmond were wondering if she was ever going to get out of dry dock. Even with fifteen hundred workmen laboring on her, progress was slow. Secretary Mallory had originally hoped to have her ready by November, but a series of tests had convinced Southern ordnance experts that the three layers of one-inch plate originally specified would not be enough armor to protect the ship's citadel, and that it would be necessary to substitute two layers of two-inch plate. It took the Tredegar people several weeks to convert their machinery to the new thickness, and the first usable armor plate did not reach Norfolk until Thanksgiving week.

Then, in January, the dockyard workforce walked out on strike. After that problem was resolved, the armor plating resumed and was finally completed at the end of the month, at about the same time as the *Monitor* was launched in Brooklyn.

In early February, with the *Merrimac* still in dry dock, the constructor, John Porter, let enough water into the dock to float the ship, so that he might judge her stability. The results were not encouraging. Her high center of gravity almost caused her to tip over, and when she was hastily righted, her bottom caught on the keel blocks that had held her in place in dry dock, and she had to be patched. Porter ordered two hundred tons of kentledge (pig iron ballast) loaded into her bilge to stabilize her, and while this helped considerably, there could be no question that the converted frigate — a compromise to begin with — was not without major problems.

Among the few unqualified successes connected with the conversion of the *Merrimac* were her guns. Lieutenant John Mercer Brooke, who had previously served under the U.S. Navy's leading artillerist, the great John Dahlgren himself, had designed rifled cannon for the bow and stern, two of 7-inch caliber, and two of 6.4-inch caliber. These cannon had been cast and bored at the Tredegar works and proved both powerful and accurate. The main battery, selected by Brooke from the ordnance captured when the Yankees abandoned the Norfolk yard, consisted of six nine-inch Dahlgrens, which were mounted three to a broadside. If the Confederates ever managed to get the *Merrimac* out of dry dock, she was going to be just as formidable a weapon as Gideon Welles feared.

Finding a crew for the *Merrimac* presented serious problems. The South had no lack of good officers — over three hundred, many of outstanding ability, had resigned their commissions in the U.S. Navy to fight for the Confederacy — but coming up with qualified deckhands, machinists, and gun crews was turning into a major headache. Eventually, General Benjamin Magruder, the army commander in charge of the defense of the peninsula, helped solve the problem by sending two hundred recruits from his own encampment near Yorktown.

On February 13, 1862, the *Merrimac* was finally launched. It was a hurried, informal affair, with no ceremony. As one foot soldier recalled it, "There were no invitations to governor and other distinguished men, no sponsor nor maid of honor, no bottle of wine, no brass band, no blowing of steam whistles, no great crowds to witness this memorable event. The launching was accomplished quietly, only officers and men stationed at the navy yard witnessed it." As with the launching of the *Monitor* a fortnight earlier, the general mood was one of skepticism and a suspicion that the ship could not possibly float with all that great weight of armor plate. When the water was let into the dock, her officers stood prudently to the side, and only a corporal and four marines were actually on board. The great ship, contrary to the fears of the unbelieving, floated out on an even keel.

By mid-February, the Union navy in New York was having problems that threatened to seriously slow down the pace of the *Monitor*'s fitting out. The most important problem related to her guns. Inherent in Ericsson's design was the understanding that only by concentrating a massive amount of power in a small space could his ship hope to stop another ironclad. To that end, he had designed the *Monitor* to carry only two guns, which were to be mounted side by side in the turret for maximum effect. Since he wanted all the destructive power he could get, he strongly urged the installation of two twelve-inch Dahlgren smoothbores, the most powerful weapons in the navy's arsenal. But in the frantic effort to get the *Monitor* ready to be turned over to the navy — they were already a month behind the one-hundred-day delivery deadline — Ericsson's stipulation of twelve-inchers was overlooked. And when Worden passed the request on to the ordnance officers at the Brooklyn Navy Yard, he was told there were none to be had. When Worden insisted, the officials assured him they were expecting a shipment of the twelve-inchers in the near future, and he put in for two of them. But the shipment never arrived, and at the last moment he and Ericsson had to settle for two eleven-inchers off the steam sloop *Dacotah*. Both guns were of recent vintage and still in good condition, and fired a 180-pound solid iron ball. While the guns were somewhat less powerful than the 12-inchers, both men hoped they might still prove to be big enough.

At 2 P.M. on February 19, the *Monitor* was officially turned over to the navy for testing. Her first cruise, a brief trip to the nearby Brooklyn Navy Yard, turned out to be little short of a disaster. No one had bothered to find out whether the *Monitor*'s propeller turned to the left or right, and as a result, when the main engine turned in the wrong direction due to a faulty valve setting, the ship's forward speed was cut to about three and a half knots. Then one of the engines driving a blower failed. It was not until 7:30 P.M. that the *Monitor* finally arrived and dropped anchor at the navy yard.

Six days later, she was officially commissioned as a fourth-rate ship in the United States Navy, and two days after that, she was deemed ready to put to sea. But the *Monitor* was an entirely new design, and it quickly became apparent that more adjustments were going to be necessary. She was hardly clear of the East River when her rudder acted up. It proved to be seriously overbalanced, and as a result, the helmsman was not able to hold the wheel once it was put over, and lost control of the ship. She rammed drunkenly into a dock and had to be ignominiously brought back to the yard under tow.

Navy officials blamed Ericsson and immediately proposed putting the *Monitor* into dry dock and fitting her out with a new rudder. But the inventor would have none of it. Dry dock would mean a month's delay, and he fiercely opposed the move.

"The *Monitor* is mine," he stormed, "and I say it shall not be done!" He was not waxing rhetorical. Because of the stringent terms of his contract, the navy had not come close to paying for the *Monitor*, and almost half of the ship still belonged to the angry Swede's syndicate. He promised to fix the problem in three days and managed to do so by interposing a system of pulleys between the tiller and the drum of the steering wheel. The stopgap measure worked well enough, but the helmsman had to turn the wheel twice as far to obtain the same angle of helm. Within a fortnight Ericsson remedied the defect permanently.

On March 3, on the occasion of the *Monitor*'s second trial run, it was discovered that even with the engines and all the machinery running smoothly, the ship would not do better than seven knots, which was less than the nine knots that Ericsson had planned or the eight knots specified in the contract. Given time, Ericsson could no doubt coax another two knots out of his engines, but that would have to wait until another day.

Time was not a luxury open to Ericsson.

On the same trial run, Chief Engineer Alban Stimers, who was on board as an unofficial member of the crew, insisted on taking charge of testing the newly installed guns. It was not the guns themselves that were in question — they had been tested many times while in the *Dacotah* — but the specially designed gun carriages that held them. These carriages had been retrofitted to adapt them to the cannon when they were installed, and Stimers, without bothering to note the nature of the alterations that had been made in order to fit such large guns in such a restricted area, turned the handwheel on gun number 1 in the wrong direction and gave the order to fire. The friction gear for the recoil of the guns failed, and the mighty Dahlgren, after emitting a deafening roar, jumped the carriage and bounced off the far wall of the turret, almost crushing a number of the gun crew. The unfazed Stimers, having totally disabled gun number 1, chalked up the mishap to somebody else's failure, and turning to gun number 2, he promptly proceeded to make the identical error, with the identical result. Remounting the two guns within the restricted confines of the turret later that day became a major engineering feat in itself.

Gideon Welles had originally hoped that the *Monitor* would be finished in time to sail up the Elizabeth River and destroy the *Merrimac* while she still lay in dry dock, but delays in readying the *Monitor* for service were making such a possibility increasingly unlikely. Then, in early February, in total disregard of the threat posed by the *Merrimac*, Assistant Secretary of the Navy Gustavus Fox began contemplating a new mission for the *Monitor*. He wired Ericsson, "Can your *Monitor* sail for the Gulf of Mexico by the 12th inst.?" The idea was to send her out to the Mississippi to aid Flag Officer David Farragut in his attack upon the forts below New Orleans, but the plan was quickly scotched when, toward the end of February, alarming news abruptly moved the focus back to Hampton Roads.

The news was brought directly into the office of Gideon Welles by a weary black woman, who had made her way through the lines on foot from Norfolk. She was a Northern spy and had been observing the progress on the conversion of the *Merrimac* on a daily basis. Now she reported that the ship was fully armored, and that the shipyard laborers were busy loading her stores and fitting her guns.

Within a few days of receiving his spy's report, Welles read a highly negative story about the new ironclad in the *Norfolk Day Book*, a local Virginia newspaper, claiming she was a complete failure. The article concluded that while she would be useless for offensive purposes, "she will make an invaluable floating battery for the protection of Norfolk, better good for something than nothing." Both Welles and Fox were convinced that the article's negative tone was proof of precisely the opposite, and that in fact the new Confederate ironclad was a greater threat than ever.

Their suspicions were confirmed on February 12, when Captain John Marston, the Union naval commander at Hampton Roads, forwarded details from a report by a Russian laborer who had been working at the Norfolk yard, flatly denying that the *Merrimac* was a failure. Captain Marston closed his dispatch by expressing disdain that the Confederates should stoop so low as to spread lies through the *Norfolk Day Book*.

By February 20, Gideon Welles no longer seemed to have any doubts as to the deployment of the *Monitor*. He sent orders to Worden to "proceed with the USS *Monitor*, under your command, to Hampton Roads, Virginia." The order might be faulted for being a bit premature — the ship still had to be put in commission, take on her crew and supplies, and undergo a number of supervised trials — but her mission was now clearly defined: to stop the *Merrimac*.

Except that she was no longer the *Merrimac*. On February 17, the Confederates had rechristened her the *Virginia*. Soon thereafter Secretary Mallory furnished her with a captain. The man he selected was Flag Officer Franklin Buchanan, a tough, sharp-witted, aggressive veteran, with a distinguished service record. Buchanan had served in the U.S. Navy for forty-six years and had been the first superintendent of the Naval Academy at Annapolis. He was the grandson of a signer of the Declaration of Independence and a lifelong Marylander, and had served with distinction in the Mexican War. By 1859 he had won appointment as captain — then the highest rank in the U.S. Navy — and was commandant of the Washington Navy Yard.

Buchanan's Southern sympathies were well-known, but even as the war clouds gathered, he had continued to enjoy wide respect in Washington. Soon after Lincoln's inauguration, the new president made it a point to attend the wedding of Buchanan's daughter and even offered to give the bride away. It was only after riots in Baltimore convinced Buchanan that Maryland was about to secede that he reluctantly resigned his commission. When Maryland failed to secede, Buchanan asked Gideon Welles to reinstate him, but the secretary refused. An embittered Buchanan retreated temporarily to his family farm in Maryland and then, growing impatient with his enforced inaction, migrated south to the Confederacy, where he was warmly received by Stephen Mallory. Once again, Gideon Welles had unwittingly provided the Confederacy with a key element of its ironcladding program.

Many in Richmond mistrusted Buchanan because he had asked for reinstatement in the U.S. Navy, but Mallory knew him to be a scrappy, wise, seasoned warrior who knew how to win battles, and who would get the most out of the strange hybrid ironclad now called the *Virginia*.

Mallory's letter to Buchanan of February 24, informing him of his appointment, provides an important insight into how the new ironclad was perceived by the man chiefly responsible for her creation. "The *Virginia* is a novelty in naval construction, is untried, and her powers unknown, and the department will not give specific orders as to her attack upon the enemy," Mallory wrote respectfully, but then immediately made it clear that his deference toward Buchanan would not preclude his making suggestions. His first is particularly noteworthy. "Her powers as a ram are regarded very formidable, and it is hoped you may be able to test them."

One of the great paradoxes of the age of steam was the return of the ram as a means of offensive war at sea. In the ancient world it had been the principal maritime weapon for centuries, and the Greeks and Romans had used it with great success, mounting huge metal rams to the bows of their galleys, which were powered by banks of oars that provided the necessary driving force to make the ram effective. When sails displaced oars, warships could no longer control their speed and course with sufficient precision, and the ram passed forever, it was thought, from the offensive tactics of naval warfare. Then the advent of steam power returned the control of speed and direction to the commander of a ship, and the ram was once again a feasible weapon. The *Virginia*, fitted with a murderous cast-iron ram that jutted out beyond her iron carapace, would be the first warship in more than a thousand years to threaten an enemy with this powerful "new," and, as Mallory suggested, highly economical weapon. "Like the bayonet charge of infantry, this mode of attack, while the most destructive, will commend itself to you in the present scarcity of ammunition. It is one also that may be rendered destructive at night against the enemy at anchor. Even without guns the ship would be formidable as a ram."

Passing on to strategic matters, Mallory reverted to his earlier visions of the all-powerful nature of ironclads. "Could you pass Old Point [i.e., Fort Monroe] and make a dashing cruise on the Potomac as far as Washington, its effect upon the public mind would be important to the cause." In closing, Mallory makes reference to the recent news of General Grant's capture of Forts Henry and Donelson in the West and ends with a fervent call for great deeds. "The condition of our country and the painful reverses we have just suffered demand our utmost exertions, and convinced as I am that the opportunity and the means for striking a decided blow for our navy are now for the first time presented, I congratulate you upon it and know that your judgment and gallantry will meet all just expectations. Action — prompt and successful action — now would be of serious importance to our cause, and with my earnest wishes for your success, and for the happiness of yourself, officers, and crew, I am, etc."

Rumors about the two ships were everywhere.

Information on the *Monitor* that reached the South tended to be highly accurate and up-to-date, because it was based on reports in the New York newspapers, which made no effort to guard the secrets of the Union's newest warship. But Southern intelligence was not always free from error. Toward the end of February, for example, Confederate General Benjamin Huger reported to his superiors that he had reliable information that the *Monitor* not only had left New York but had arrived in Hampton Roads, which was of course wildly off the mark. The Yankees were no better informed. On February 28, Union Captain Henry Van Brunt, of the steam frigate *Minnesota*, anchored off Newport News, wrote a gossipy letter to his old friend, Flag Officer Louis M. Goldsborough, describing the deceptive calm at Hampton Roads. "We have nothing new here; all is quiet. The *Merrimac* is still invisible to us, but reports say she is ready to come out. I sincerely wish she would; I am quite tired of hearing of her."

The one thing on which both intelligence systems could agree was that at some as yet undetermined point in time, the two ironclads were bound to confront one another in Hampton Roads.

Interest in the expected battle was not limited to the combatants. In the middle of February three French warships appeared in the Roads. Warships, because they were vessels of state, and did not carry cargo, were not subject to the blockade. The squadron was ostensibly traveling on diplomatic business, but its commanding officer, the marquis de Montaignac, made it clear he was interested in observing any possible military activity as well. He requested permission from the Union naval commander for one of his ships to anchor halfway between Fort Monroe and Newport News Point, so that he and his officers might more clearly observe any action should it develop.

The French took pains to maintain a diplomatic evenhandedness and to deal with both sides equally. While the response of the Union commanders to the French overtures was cordial, that of the Confederates was positively effusive. The leaders in Richmond saw an opportunity to curry favor and possibly convince France to reconsider her strict neutrality toward the South. Orders went out to the navy command at Norfolk to treat the visitors with utmost deference. When the marquis expressed curiosity at a report in the *New York Times* that the *Merrimac* "was drawing so much water that she could not get out even if she was ready for sea," Southern officials laughingly assured him that the newspaper's report was based on a deliberately deceptive story, and that the ironclad was in fact almost ready for action.

When the French commodore requested a tour of the Southern ironclad, the Confederates eagerly agreed. On the appointed day, a large party of French officers was escorted up the Elizabeth River by their Southern hosts and treated to a day of ceremony and festivities, capped by a carefully conducted inspection of the newly christened *Virginia*. The guests, almost all of whom had served in the far more sophisticated *Gloire* or her ironclad sisters, were polite but diplomatically noncommittal in their comments about the *Virginia*, which, by their hosts' own admission, was something of a makeshift compromise. They may well have found the ship's battery impressive, but it is likely that they also noticed that the rough-and-ready conditions on board left something to be desired.

Certainly those who had to endure those conditions made note of them. "We are living aboard, and are as uncomfortable as possible," noted the ship's executive officer, Lieutenant Catesby ap Rogers Jones, disconsolately. "There has not been a dry spot aboard of her, leaks everywhere — mechanics are at work at a thousand things which should have been done months ago." Jones's comments are important, because they present a candid assessment of the ship at this final stage of her conversion, by an experienced officer who was making no attempt at either dissimulation, to confound the North, or exaggerated glorification, to comfort the South.

But if the *Virginia* was not quite ready for action, her captain was no longer willing to wait. Buchanan was acutely aware that the time element, always crucial, was becoming more so every day. The *Monitor* might show up momentarily, and her presence in Hampton Roads would change the picture entirely. In the meantime, all those wooden Yankee warships sat in the Roads unprotected, and the opportunity to attack them grew more compelling with every passing day.

On March 4, he moved into the captain's quarters on board ship and took formal command, ordering most of the workmen ashore, and retaining only those busy with the most vital details. "This vessel is about to face the enemy just as soon as I can get her there," he announced.

Commodore Forrest, in charge of the navy yard, protested vehemently. He was responsible for the *Virginia* as long as she remained in dry dock, and he pointed out that most of her gun port shutters had not been fitted and there was still work to be done on the underwater plating. Buchanan brushed aside his objections. "I mean to try her against the enemy, sir!" he declared emphatically. "There will be time to complete the shutters and armor after we have proved her in action!"

On March 6, 1862, Gideon Welles, acting with the same almost inexplicable lack of understanding that had caused him to bring about the *Merrimac* crisis in the first place, decided at the last minute to change the *Monitor*'s orders still again. General McClellan had convinced him that the ironclad might prove useful in helping him clear the Potomac for one of his projected troop movements, and the secretary had returned to his office and sent a telegram to New York countermanding his own orders of February 20, and summarily ordering Worden to bypass Hampton Roads entirely, and to bring the *Monitor* directly to Washington.

In the light of subsequent events, Welles's order came close to being an act of criminal stupidity. Had it been carried out, he would undoubtedly have been subjected to public disgrace and possibly impeachment. As it transpired, he was saved from such a fate by fortuitous circumstances beyond his control. Two hours before his message reached New York, the *Monitor* had left the Brooklyn Navy Yard for the last time, passed the Narrows and cleared Sandy Hook, and, in the company of a tugboat and two gunboats, set out on her journey to immortality. She would remain out of communication with the shore until she reached the Chesapeake.

9

THE VOYAGE SOUTH

For all her innovative design, and for all of John Ericsson's protestations to the contrary, the *Monitor* was never truly designed to be an ocean-going vessel. Even Captain Worden, who was an enthusiastic believer in his ship's potential, recognized the need to exercise a certain caution in her command. He received his final orders to proceed to Hampton Roads on Tuesday, March 4, and was eager to get under way from New York, but when a severe coastal storm unexpectedly blew in, he chose the course of prudence and postponed his departure until the winds finally moderated two days later and he judged it was safe to take the *Monitor* to sea.

On the morning of March 6, a Thursday, Worden ordered his deckhands to make fast a four-hundred-foot towline to the steam tug *Seth Low*, and at 11 A.M., the USS *Monitor*, under tow but powered by her own engines as well, pulled away from the Brooklyn Navy Yard for the last time and set to sea. The two vessels were accompanied by the steam gunboats *Currituck* and *Sachem*, and by 4 P.M. the little flotilla of rather insignificant-looking naval vessels rounded Sandy Hook and turned south along the New Jersey coast.

The maiden cruise began in unseasonably pleasant weather, and the *Monitor*'s first taste of the open sea was such that Worden and his crew had an opportunity to get to know their strange new ship and familiarize themselves with her workings under what might be considered ideal circumstances.

There were a total of fifty-eight men on board, including thirteen officers and forty-five men of various ratings. All were volunteers, because the navy was reluctant to assign personnel arbitrarily to such a novel and untested vessel. Five of the ship's officers and twenty-one of her men were defined as being of the line, responsible for the handling of the *Monitor* and her guns, while another five officers and seventeen men were responsible for the engines and other mechanical operations. The remaining ten men — including the paymaster, surgeon, clerk, storekeepers, cooks, and stewards — were not directly involved in the working of the ship but were necessary to the general organization of life on board.

The advent of steam had created a predictable snobbery in the navies of the world. Line officers, who held the traditional naval responsibilities for running a ship, and who operated for the most part on deck, tended to look down on the new class of engineering officers, who generally worked below and who as often as not were covered in coal dust and machine oil and carried with them the perpetual odor of smoke and fly ash. It could not have escaped the notice of anyone in the luxurious wardroom of the *Monitor*, where the officers met for meals, that in their new ship all duty stations were below deck, and since the ship carried no means of propelling herself through the water except those presided over by the engineers, there was no place for snobbery of any sort.

The most important member of the crew, with the exception of Worden himself, was the fifty-eighth man on board, a supernumerary not even officially assigned to the ship, Chief Engineer Alban C. Stimers. Stimers was the man Gideon Welles had selected to supervise the construction of the *Monitor* on behalf of the navy, and who was now accompanying the ship to Hampton Roads as an observer and general expert.

The *Monitor*'s first night at sea was as calm and uneventful as the first day. She rode easily atop the waves, with little water breaking over her low deck. Alban Stimers assigned members of the crew to check everywhere for leaks, but the only ones discovered, on the deck and at the forward main hatch, were of a minor nature and easily handled by the pumps. After sunset, the moon rose in the east, and from the hatches atop the turret it was possible to make out the green running lights of the *Currituck* and *Sachem*, steaming easily off the port bow. All was serene, and in the wardroom several of the officers, who were enjoying a nightcap after the evening meal, exchanged congratulations on their good fortune in finding such accommodating weather. Stimers, in a report to Ericsson, wrote: "I never saw a vessel more buoyant or less shocked, than she was yesterday. There has not been sufficient movement to disturb a wine glass setting on the table."

But the Atlantic in winter is nothing if not unpredictable, and by the following dawn the weather had changed radically. A light gale had worked up from the west, storm clouds gathered overhead, and the smooth seas turned choppy and angry. William F. Keeler, the paymaster, awoke to discover that the captain and the ship's surgeon were suffering from extreme seasickness, and had been moved to the top of the turret to revive in the fresh air.

The weather continued to deteriorate until the seas were breaking over the deck with such force that the whole ship shook. The power of the increasing storm started leaks in many parts of the ship and brought to light a dreadful error made by the men at the Brooklyn Navy Yard charged with the responsibility for preparing the *Monitor* for sea. Ericsson had designed the turret so that it would fit snugly into the brass ring in the deck, forming a virtually watertight seal, but navy yard officials had ignored his instructions to let the great weight of the turret serve as its own seal, and had deliberately jacked up the turret on wedges and stuffed a gasket of oakum — bits of old rope — around the entire base. The impact of the waves had dislodged the oakum, creating a circular opening sixty-three feet in circumference, into which the sea, now raging in the midst of a full-scale storm, poured in from all sides. The pumps were unable to keep up with the flow, and the ship was soon in danger of foundering.

The *Monitor*'s executive officer, Lieutenant Samuel Dana Greene, described how "the berth-deck hatch leaked in spite of all we could do, and the water came down under the turret like a waterfall." Other problems arose as a result of design faults in the ship. The little pilothouse, the small, boxlike structure that rose out of the forward deck near the bow, was totally unprotected. Greene described how the water "would strike the pilot-house and go over the turret in beautiful curves, and it came through the narrow eye-holes in the pilot-house with such force as to knock the helmsman completely round from the wheel."

Ericsson had designed the *Monitor* so that she would require no smokestack, but for the voyage south he had added a temporary six-foot funnel to protect against high seas, and soon the waves were breaking over it, revealing another design error. Seawater poured into the engine room from the air-intake vents on deck and soaked the leather belts that carried power off the engines to turn the blower fans. The moisture stretched and loosened the belts, and the fans, which were designed to pull in fresh air and expel foul air, stopped turning. Then one of the belts snapped, and all hell broke loose. With no artificial draft of fresh air to feed the fires, the engines stopped, and choking fumes of carbon dioxide filled the engine room. The entire rear half of the ship became a deathtrap.

Both Stimers and the *Monitor*'s chief engineer, the felicitously named Isaac Newton, tried desperately to get the blowers working again, with little success. "The fires burned with a sickly blaze," Stimers wrote later, "converting all the air in the engine and fire rooms into carbonic-acid-gas, a few inhalations of which are sufficient to destroy animal life." He ordered everybody out of the engine compartment and stayed behind to try to get a blower working again. In minutes, he was almost overcome. Reeling blindly up the companionway, he barely managed to claw his way to the turret before collapsing on the deck. The engine room filled with poison gas, and because someone had left a hatch open, it began spreading through the rest of the ship.

The only sources of fresh air below deck were now the turret hatch and the narrow observation slit in the pilothouse, and the crew was as much in danger of asphyxiation as of drowning. The ship was taking on water at a frightful rate, and the pumps that were designed to get rid of it were now useless, because they were dependent on the same boiler fires that were failing for lack of air.

Seawater sloshed through the berth deck from end to end. With the steam pumps inoperable, Lieutenant Greene tried to set up hand pumps, but they, too, failed. Out of desperation, he organized a bucket brigade that wound from the berth deck to the top of the turret, which probably contributed little to the safety of the ship but served to steady the crew.

Greene tried to summon help by flying the flag upside down in a distress signal, but the *Currituck* and *Sachem* were as helpless as the ironclad and could do nothing. Finally he managed to get the *Seth Low* to pull toward shore, several miles to the west, where the sea was smoother, and after a difficult progress that took almost five hours, they managed to reach safer waters.

In the calmer seas, Stimers and his men were finally able to repair the blower belts and clear the deadly gas from below. With ventilation restored, he was able to restart the boilers, and soon the steady thumping of the engines sent a reassuring message throughout the ship. Slowly but surely, the throbbing pumps got rid of the seawater, and a soggy but seaworthy *Monitor* resumed her voyage.

The second evening was as clear and beautiful as the previous night, and those who could find a dry place to rest tried to get some sleep. Shortly after midnight, an exhausted Lieutenant Greene lay down for a brief nap when he was startled awake by "the most infernal noise I ever heard in my life." The *Monitor* was once again in peril. As Greene would describe the situation a few days later: "We were just passing a shoal, and the sea suddenly became rough and right ahead. It came up with tremendous force through our anchor well and forced the air through our hawse-pipe where the chain comes, and then the water would rush through in a perfect stream, clear to our berth deck, over the wardroom table. The noise resembled the death groans of twenty men, and was the most dismal, awful sound I have ever heard."

The same individuals who had unwittingly endangered the *Monitor* by deliberately jacking up the turret and inserting oakum in the base had with equal blindness ignored Ericsson's instructions to plug the aperture — the hawse pipe — through which the anchor chain passed. As a result, seawater had poured in, accompanied by the "dismal, awful sound" of forced air, which turned the pipe into a huge, discordant flute.

Greene's ordeal was far from over. "Of course the captain and myself were on our feet in a moment, and endeavored to stop the hawse-pipe. We succeeded partially, but now the water began to come down our blowers again, and we feared the same accident that happened in the afternoon. We tried to hail the tugboat, but the wind being dead ahead they could not hear us, and we had no way of signaling them. . . .

"We began to think the *Monitor* would never see daylight. We watched carefully every drop of water that went down the blowers, and sent continually to ask the fireman how they were going. His only answer was 'Slowly,' but could not be kept going much longer unless the water could

142

be kept from coming down. The sea was washing completely over the decks, and it was dangerous for a man to go on them, so we could do nothing to the blowers. In the midst of all this our wheel-ropes jumped off the steering-wheel (owing to the pitching of the ship), and became jammed. She now began to sheer about at an awful rate, and we thought our hawser would certainly part. Fortunately it was new, and held on well. In the course of half an hour we freed our wheel-ropes, and now the blowers were the only difficulty. About three o'clock Saturday A.M. the sea became a little smoother, though still rough, and going down our blowers somewhat."

By 8 A.M. Saturday, March 8, the *Seth Low* had once again hauled them into more sheltered waters, and the men were able to find some breakfast. For a second time in as many days, the ship had been saved from near-certain disaster. The berth deck, illuminated by the pale morning sunlight that filtered in through the thick glass prisms inserted into the deck above, was wet and slippery, and water still leaked in through the turret and overhead hatches, but the ship was safe, and the engines beat strongly. They were by this time off the low sandy coast of Maryland's eastern shore, and at noon they passed Cape Charles and entered Chesapeake Bay. Two hours later, the frayed and worn hawser that held the *Monitor* to the *Seth Low* finally parted, but in the relatively calm waters of the bay it was a simple enough matter to repair, and about 3 P.M. they sighted and passed Cape Henry, on the southern side of the Chesapeake's mouth. They were now about fifteen miles from their destination.

While still in sight of Cape Henry, but before the great mass of Fort Monroe loomed over the western horizon, the men on deck and in the top of the turret began to hear, in the distance, over the regular thumping of the machinery, a muffled and not immediately identifiable sound. It was apparently gunfire, coming from the direction of Hampton Roads. Lieutenant Keeler climbed to the turret top and searched the horizon. "As we neared the land," he wrote later, "clouds of smoke could be seen hanging over it in the direction of the Fortress, & as we approached still nearer little black spots could occasionally be seen, suddenly springing in the air, remaining stationary for a moment or two & then gradually expanding into a larger white cloud." Some of the veterans on board identified the black spots as shells bursting in air. The news electrified the exhausted officers and men.

Impatient to find out what was happening, Worden hailed the first pilot boat he could find. As it drew alongside, and the pilot stepped down to the deck — which was undoubtedly for him a novel and unexpected means of embarking — the officers of the *Monitor* crowded around him to hear the latest intelligence. Even though they had guessed the nature of the gunfire, the news still came as a shock: The rebels had finally unleashed the *Merrimac*, the pilot explained excitedly. She had come down the Elizabeth River that morning, a deadly and invincible scourge, and was in the process of destroying the entire U.S. Navy blockading squadron, ship by ship.

10

THE *VIRGINIA* ATTACKS

March 4, the day that John Worden received his final orders to proceed to Hampton Roads, was the same day that Flag Officer Franklin Buchanan moved on board the *Virginia* while she was still undergoing her final refitting in the Norfolk yard, and took formal command. Old Buck knew precisely what he wanted to do with his new ship, and he knew how he wanted to do it. He would break the blockade's stranglehold on the James River, and open the door to Richmond, by destroying the Union flotilla that had controlled Hampton Roads since the war began.

His immediate targets were the USS *Congress* and the USS *Cumberland*, both of which were sailing ships, without steam power, and therefore extremely vulnerable. Once he had disposed of those two, circumstances would dictate where he would strike next. There would be plenty of choices. Also in the Roads were two sister ships of the *Merrimac*, the steam frigates *Minnesota* and *Roanoke*, as well as the steamer *Cambridge*, the store ship *Brandywine*, the sloop of war *St. Lawrence*, three coal ships, a hospital ship, five tugboats, a side-wheeler steamer, and a sailing bark, altogether a large, well-manned squadron mounting a total of 188 guns. Against this powerful force Buchanan had the ten-gun *Virginia*, along with a ragtag assortment of castoffs, including the twelve-gun *Patrick Henry*, the two-gun *Jamestown*, and the *Teaser*, *Beaufort*, and *Raleigh*, all of one gun, for a total of twenty-seven guns.

Buchanan explained his plan in a letter to Lieutenant John R. Tucker, the senior officer of the James River Squadron, whose small flotilla was imprisoned by the Union guns at the river's mouth.

"It is my intention," he wrote, "if no accident occurs to this ship to prevent it, to appear before the enemy off Newport News at daylight on Friday next. You will . . . be prepared to join me. My object is first to destroy the frigates *Congress* and *Cumberland*, if possible, and then turn my attention to the destruction of the battery on shore and the gunboats." Although Buchanan framed his ambitions with a self-deprecatory "if possible," the letter is remarkable for its hubris. To announce officially before going into battle that he intended to single-handedly destroy not one but two frigates showed an awesome faith in his new ironclad.

His executive officer, Lieutenant Jones, was not nearly so sanguine about the *Virginia*'s prospects. He had been at Norfolk since the beginning of the conversion, and for months he had been dogging the navy yard constructor, demanding better workmanship, greater efficiencies, more armor. On March 5, the day after Buchanan moved on board and only two days before the *Virginia*'s scheduled departure, he was still concerned. "The ship is too light, or I should say, she is not sufficiently protected below the water," he wrote privately. "Our draft will be a foot less than was first intended, yet I was this morning ordered not to put any more ballast in fear of [the ship scraping] the bottom. The eaves of the roof [the armored citadel] will not be more than six inches immersed, which in smooth water will not be enough, a slight ripple would leave it bare except the one-inch iron that extends some feet below. We are least protected where we most need it. The constructor should have put in six inches where we now have one."

But if the *Virginia*'s protective skirt was less than adequate, Buchanan chose not to worry about it. If matters went as he anticipated, any deficiencies in armor plating would be unimportant. Surprise was the key. He planned to slip down the Elizabeth River on Thursday night and attack at dawn on Friday, March 7, steaming across Hampton Roads under cover of darkness and catching the Yankees unawares at first light. When a severe gale materialized — the same storm that almost sank the *Monitor* off the New Jersey coast — he was forced to postpone his departure for twenty-four hours. Then his plans for total surprise had to be abandoned, when his pilots told him they could not navigate the river at night. Buchanan was disappointed but not overly concerned. His targets, he knew, would wait for him and would undoubtedly remain where they were until it suited him to attack.

Much later, it came to be recognized that Buchanan's postponement changed naval history. If the *Virginia* had steamed out on the seventh, as originally planned, she would have had two full days to complete her work of devastation, and by the time the *Monitor* reached Hampton Roads on the evening of the eighth, he would have returned in the *Virginia* to Norfolk, where she would have been shielded by an impregnable series of batteries built into the river on both banks. The confrontation between the *Monitor* and the *Virginia* might never have taken place.

During the day's enforced inactivity, Buchanan ordered a final shipment of gunpowder stored in the *Virginia*'s magazines, giving him nearly eighteen thousand pounds of the precious stuff. Then, because it was thought that a coating of tallow on the ironcladding might cause cannonballs to skid off the slanted wall of the citadel, he had his crew slosh over the surface of the ship as much pork fat as would stick to the iron plates.

A letter from Secretary Mallory to Buchanan dated March 7 dramatically expresses the high hopes for the *Virginia* held by the South, and incorporates the worst fears of the North: "I submit for your consideration the attack of New York by the *Virginia*. Can the *Virginia* steam to New York and attack and burn the city? She can, I doubt not, pass Old Point safely, and in good weather and a smooth sea she could doubtless go to New York. Once in the bay she could shell and burn the city and the shipping. Such an event would eclipse all the glories of all the combats of the sea, would place every man in it preeminently high, and would strike a blow from which the enemy could never recover. Peace would inevitably follow. Bankers would withdraw their capital from the city, the Brooklyn navy-yard and its magazines and all the lower part of the city would be destroyed, and such an event, by a single ship, would do more to achieve an immediate independence than would the results of many campaigns.

"Can the ship go there? Please give me your views."

Old Buck may have wondered if Mallory was serious. Much as Buchanan relished the opportunity to take the *Virginia* into action in the sheltered waters of Hampton Roads, he would not have trusted her in the Atlantic, even on a calm day. But, of course, that was not the kind of information one wanted to commit to paper.

On Saturday the weather broke, and shortly before 11 A.M. Buchanan summarily dismissed all the navy yard workmen laboring on the *Virginia* and sent them ashore, and ordered his officers to prepare for departure. The constructor's office protested that the steel shutters for the *Virginia*'s gunports were still lying on the dock waiting to be installed, but Buchanan ignored their arguments. He did not intend to wait another day before launching his attack on the Union forces controlling the Roads.

The fact that Buchanan planned to take the *Virginia* directly into action was a secret known to only two or three officers. Everyone else in the navy yard, including virtually her entire 260-man crew, assumed he planned only a practice run for his untried ship. In the last minutes before departure, he let Chief Engineer H. Ashton Ramsay in on the secret. "Ramsay," Buchanan asked casually, "what would happen to your engines and boilers if there should be a collision?"

The engineer assured him that the machinery was properly braced, and that a collision would not harm it. It was the answer Buchanan wanted.

"I am going to ram the *Cumberland*," he confided. "I am told she has the new rifled guns, the only ones in their whole fleet we have cause to fear. The moment we are out in the Roads, I'm going to make right for her and ram her."

By 11 A.M. the tide was at half-flood, which meant there was now just barely enough water to float the *Virginia*'s deep twenty-two-foot draft on her way downriver. The tide would continue to rise until 1:30 P.M., and Buchanan was determined to be in the Roads by high tide, where he would need every bit of the water's depth to maneuver in the shallows off Newport News.

Buchanan ordered his red ensign hoist and prepared to cast off. The *Virginia's* weak and unreliable engines churned loudly, and laboriously pulled her into the river's mainstream. Her little consorts, the *Beaufort* and the *Raleigh*, inched her slowly around until she pointed downstream, and at last the *Virginia*, a great iron mountain smelling of pig fat, her angled sides glistening in the sunlight, began to make her way, at times with painful slowness like an arthritic queen, past the city of Norfolk and downriver to the Roads. Lining the riverbanks, thousands of soldiers and civilians crowded the shore, some cheering the brave sight, some standing in silent awe at the great, dark behemoth, with a Confederate flag snapping bravely from the sternmost point on her citadel, as she proceeded slowly north to the mouth of the river. As she passed, many of the onlookers made hurried plans to get to Sewell's Point, where they hoped to watch the great ironclad chase down the Yankees.

If those on shore were confident of victory, some of the officers on board, who knew the facts, must have suffered a momentary twinge of trepidation. The *Virginia* was nowhere near as fit for battle as she might appear from a distance. Her engines were notoriously unreliable, and her steering gear insufficient. Her guns had not been fired since installation. Her crew were for the most part soldiers recruited from the army, who had no idea what they were there to do. Many of them had never stood on a deck until that morning.

The trip downriver would be the last opportunity to get something to eat, and Buchanan ordered the boatswain to pipe all hands to dinner. Chief Engineer Ramsay prepared to join the other officers in the wardroom, where they were enjoying some cold tongue and biscuit, but changed his mind when he saw the ship's assistant surgeon at the other end of the dining table, laying out surgical instruments and lint for bandages in preparation for the action to come. "The sight took away my appetite," he explained.

The *Virginia*'s highly erratic steering was not to be trusted, and about two miles below Norfolk she took a tow from the *Beaufort* to help her round a bend in the river. As the great vessel juddered laboriously to starboard, the men in the pilothouse saw the full extent of Hampton Roads opening up before them in the distance. Dead ahead, beyond the mouth of the river, and framed by Sewell's Point to the east and Craney Island to the west, lay the waters for which she had been with such arduous difficulty rebuilt to conquer. On the horizon they could make out the great mass of Fort Monroe, and a few points to port, the anchorage of the *Cumberland* and *Congress*.

It was now about 12:30, one hour before high tide.

In the many accounts of the events of that Saturday, all agree that the weather was unusually beautiful for early March, clear and bright, with a gentle breeze from the northwest.

The first Union forces to spot the *Virginia* were probably the lookouts at Fort Monroe. Around noon, long before the ironclad actually exited the mouth of the Elizabeth, soldiers on the ramparts noted signs of activity across the Roads, which might indicate a large steam vessel coming down the river. General John E. Wool, in command of the fort, immediately telegraphed a warning to the batteries at Newport News, and it was a little later, about 12:40, that the soldiers manning the guns directly across from the mouth of the Elizabeth saw a column of heavy black smoke rising from the direction of Sewell's Point and guessed that the great ironclad for which they had been waiting so many months was at last entering the Roads.

The crews of the *Cumberland* and the *Congress*, the two Yankee ships anchored off Newport News, had spent the morning washing clothes, and following navy custom, had hung their laundry out to dry on the rigging, with white garments to starboard and blues to port. The lifeboats of both ships were hanging from lowered booms that morning, ready to move people to and from the shore, just three hundred yards away.

A few minutes after the army batteries spotted the *Virginia*, the duty quartermaster on the *Congress* noticed the same telltale black smoke. Turning to a nearby officer on deck, he said, "I wish

154

you would take the glass and have a look over there, sir. I believe that thing is a-comin' down at last."

The lookouts on the *Cumberland*, anchored two hundred yards away, saw the same thing, but as the *Virginia* was still in the river, and obscured behind Craney Island, they could not be certain of the stranger's identity.

There was a mad scurry aboard both ships as the washing was whipped off the rigging, the topsails set, the lifeboats secured or sent in to the land, the guns run out, and the decks quickly strewn with sand. This last was to ensure that in case of battle, the gun crews would continue to have sure footing when the blood from the dead and wounded turned the decks into a gory and slippery nightmare.

Both ships were old, built before the age of steam, and dependent entirely upon their sails. Now their officers called out frantically to the nearby steam tugs to tow them into battle positions.

Several miles distant, off Old Point Comfort, on the far side of Fort Monroe and actually outside the Roads, the two large Union steam frigates *Minnesota* and *Roanoke*, sister ships of forty guns each, lay at anchor, as yet unaware of the dramatic turn of events. At 1:08 a lookout vessel stationed in the Roads raised signal flag 551, alerting everyone that the enemy was approaching. Almost immediately the *Minnesota*'s captain ordered her boilers fired up, while the *Roanoke*, which was partially disabled with a broken propeller shaft, frantically signaled for a tug to move her down to where the action seemed likely to occur.

At ten minutes after the hour, the *Virginia* finally made her appearance. As one Yankee participant described it, "Pretty soon that great black thing, different from any vessel ever seen before, poked her nose around Sewell's Point."

Once in sight of the enemy, Buchanan came down from the pilothouse and addressed the crew assembled on the gun deck, revealing for the first time that the *Virginia* would soon be going into action. "Sailors," he proclaimed, "in a few minutes you will have the long-expected opportunity to show your devotion to your country and our cause. Remember that you are about to strike for your country and your homes, your wives and your children." Many of the men had already guessed the truth, and all met it with good cheer and returned to their guns.

Once in the Roads proper, Buchanan ordered the *Beaufort* to ease the *Virginia* around to port, so that she faced directly toward Newport News and the two Yankee warships he had previously targeted. He could see smoke pouring out of the *Minnesota*'s stack just beyond Old Point Comfort, as she and the *Roanoke* prepared to come to the rescue of the ships at Newport News.

A Union tug, the *Zouave*, steamed briskly toward Pig Point to verify the identity of the stranger. "It did not take us long to find out," her captain reported, "for we had not gone over two miles when we saw what to all appearances looked like the roof of a very big barn belching forth smoke as from a chimney on fire." There could be no question that she was the long-feared Confederate ironclad, and the captain ordered his men to start firing at her with the boat's thirty-pounder Parrott rifle. The *Zouave* poured a half dozen shots at the *Virginia* with absolutely no effect, before she was called back to Newport News to help with the two sailing ships. Hers were the first shots in the battle.

It was now about 1:30, and the water in the Roads stood at high tide.

With a sense of inevitability in her movements, the *Virginia* plowed slowly but unfalteringly forward. All over the Roads, small boats were scurrying out of harm's way, "like chickens scattering before a hawk," as one observer put it.

By now, the *Virginia* was receiving fire from both the *Cumberland* and the *Congress*, as well as the shore batteries at Newport News, but she made no reply. It was not until 2 P.M. that the *Beaufort* fired the first round from the Confederate side, a thirty-two-pound rifle shot, aimed at the *Congress*.

On both the northern and southern shores of the Roads, twenty thousand soldiers, split evenly between the opposing armies, watched with fascination and dread as the *Virginia*, an awesome dark monster, pushed relentlessly toward her prey at a steady, unwavering six knots, like some terribly slow but undeviating nemesis. She fairly bristled with guns, but at this point in the action only two of them, those mounted on the forward face of the citadel, could be aimed at the *Cumberland*. As the distance between the two ships shrunk to less than a mile, Buchanan ordered the seven-inch Brooke rifle bow gun to commence firing. The first shell hit the *Cumberland* square, exploding in a shower of lethal flying splinters that wounded several marines. The *Cumberland* returned fire with a full broadside, to no effect. The second shell from the *Virginia* burst in the midst of a gun crew struggling to reload, killing every man except the powder boy and the gun captain, who lost both arms at the shoulder. The *Cumberland*'s entire starboard battery, divided into fore and aft divisions, began firing as fast as crews could reload and aim, but their shells proved ineffectual against the *Virginia*'s armor, and the great hulking vessel continued its steady and unswerving course, its forward gun wreaking havoc with every shot. The Yankee dead were dragged unceremoniously to the port side and stacked up for later burial. Lieutenant Thomas O. Selfridge, commanding the forward division, watched in grim horror as the devastation mounted. The first and second captains of every one of his guns were either killed or wounded, and he was reduced to moving from gun to gun, placing primers in the breech vents of each cannon and firing them as fast as the decimated crews could reload.

By 2:30 the *Virginia* was only three hundred yards from the *Cumberland*. The *Congress*, which had now found the range, was firing broadside after broadside at the *Virginia* with a singular lack of effect. Buchanan did not even seem to notice. His attention was fixed on his quarry. But as the *Virginia* moved parallel to the *Congress*, her starboard gun crews, which had been standing by with nothing to shoot at, suddenly found a target and unleashed the full fury of their broadside of nine-inch Dahlgrens. The effect of the first salvo was devastating. One of the *Virginia*'s shells struck the carriage of gun number 7 on board the *Congress*, killing or wounding the entire crew and dismounting the gun. Other shots pierced the hull, starting fires that threatened to reach the powder magazine and blow the ship sky-high.

On came the *Virginia* toward the *Cumberland*, "weird and mysterious, like some devilish and superhuman monster, or the horrid creation of a nightmare," reported a Boston newspaperman. The Yankee gunners fought bravely, but their shots "struck and glanced off, having no more effect than peas from a pop-gun."

The *Cumberland*'s pilot, A. B. Smith, described the *Virginia* as looking "like a huge, half submerged crocodile." She was now close enough for everyone to see her most devastating weapon. "At her prow I could see the iron ram projecting, straight forward, somewhat above the water's edge, and apparently a mass of iron."

The moment of impact was almost lost in the noise and activity of the ongoing battle. The great iron ram, propelled by the huge mass of ironclad ship behind it, and moving inexorably at six knots, ripped through the fragile torpedo barriers set out to protect the ship from enemy sea mines while at anchor, and tore into the side of the *Cumberland* below the waterline, leaving a gaping hole large enough to drive a horse and cart through. It was a mortal wound. For all the terrible damage it caused, the ramming was almost unperceived on board the *Virginia*, where the men on the gun deck could not see the enemy ship or know its distance, and where one of the officers noted only a slight jarring sensation. Even on the deck of the *Cumberland*, the actual ramming did not cause immediate concern. "The shock of the collision was of course perceptible, but was not violent," a survivor remembered.

But there was no way to overlook the immediate aftermath of the ramming. Seawater poured into the seven-foot hole, and the *Cumberland* began to sink by the starboard bow. And now suddenly it was the *Virginia* that was in peril, for her ram had caught in the timbers of her victim, and she was in danger of being dragged under by the *Cumberland*. Desperately, Chief Engineer Ramsay threw the *Virginia*'s engines into reverse, forcing them to the limits of their potential until the ship was shaking in every fiber. But still the ram stuck, and the *Virginia* could not break away. Finally, it was the early-afternoon tide that saved her, forcing the *Virginia* up against the side of the *Cumberland* until the two ships were almost parallel, at which point the great ram twisted and broke off from the bow of the *Virginia*, freeing her from the *Cumberland*'s death grip. "Like the wasp, we could sting but once, leaving the sting in the wound," Ramsay wrote.

The doomed *Cumberland*, already sinking, continued to fight. The Confederate Lieutenant John Taylor Wood, on board the *Virginia*, recalled respectfully, "No ship was ever fought more gallantly." For nearly half an hour after the ramming she remained afloat, and during that time, she and the *Virginia* traded close-range broadsides of terrible ferocity, which produced, in the case of the *Virginia*, sickening slaughter aboard the Yankee ship, and in the case of the *Cumberland*, a heartbreaking, pointless waste of lives. Three times the *Cumberland* managed to hurl a full broadside of eighty-pound solid shot from her eleven guns, but the *Virginia*'s tough hide repulsed every attack. At one point, toward the end, the barrage from the *Cumberland* reached such a pitch of concentration that the heat from her shot set fire to the pig fat that covered the *Virginia*. "It seemed she was literally frying from one end to the other," Confederate Lieutenant Hardin B. Littlepage recalled. One of the *Virginia*'s gunners, John Hunt, turned to another, Jack Cronin, and called out, "Jack, don't this smell like hell?" Cronin agreed, and called back, "And I think we'll all be there in a few minutes!"

Around 3:35 the *Cumberland* gave a sudden lurch to port as her berth deck went under. The unexpected shift caused one of her guns to break loose from its tackle and crush an unwary sailor against the port rail. Her commanding officer refused to surrender, but it was pointless to continue the fight, and he gave the order to abandon ship. What remained of her crew jumped into the water and struck out for shore. Rescue boats immediately set out to meet them.

"She went down bravely, with her colors flying," wrote the *Virginia*'s executive officer with admiration. The water was so shallow that when the *Cumberland* settled to the bottom, the top of her masts, with her flag still snapping in the breeze, remained above the waves, a memorial to the 121 dead victims of the terrifying and invincible fighting machine that had emerged two hours earlier to take command of Hampton Roads.

Buchanan was acutely aware that it was now two hours past high tide, and he was eager to get to the *Congress*, but his ship was so unwieldy and difficult to manage that he could not get her to face in the right direction. He had to head away from the fight, into the mouth of the James River, to find the room to turn her around. Once again her escorts, the *Beaufort* and *Raleigh*, like two mahouts trying to guide a recalcitrant elephant, had to do most of the turning. While so engaged, the three vessels were exposed to the Union Army's land batteries at Newport News, but in spite of heavy fire they managed to complete the maneuver without incident. Now, joined by three little warships from the James River Squadron, the *Virginia* turned east again to continue the attack.

The men in the *Congress* had watched with dread foreboding as the *Virginia* deliberately rammed and sank the *Cumberland*, and her commanding officer, unaware that the Confederate ship had lost her ram in the action, was determined that Buchanan would not have the opportunity to attack the *Congress* in the same fashion. With the help of the tug *Zouave*, he deliberately beached his ship as close as possible to the army batteries on shore, in water too shallow for the *Virginia* to reach. It was an intelligent and brave move, but unfortunately for the *Congress*, she was not able to beach herself parallel to the shore, which might have allowed her to bring her full broadside to bear. Instead, her highly vulnerable stern was exposed seaward, with only chase guns to protect her.

Almost certainly, painful thoughts must have passed through Buchanan's mind as he approached the helpless wooden Union warship. Like many American families, the Buchanans had been divided by the war. He knew that his brother McKean Buchanan was paymaster aboard the *Congress*, and that by ordering the attack, he might well be ordering his own brother's death.

The only thing that now stood between Buchanan and assured victory was the possibility that one of the steam frigates he had earlier spotted heading toward Newport News might get there before he had finished off the *Congress,* but a quick glance to the east showed him there was little chance of that. The *Roanoke,* which had grounded earlier in her hurry to get to the scene of action, had since that time freed herself and turned tail toward Fort Monroe. The *Minnesota,* about a mile and a half away, was solidly grounded and appeared incapable of extricating herself.

The nearest Buchanan dared bring his ship to the *Congress* was two hundred yards, but as it turned out, that was close enough. The trapped Union frigate could bring only two guns to bear on the *Virginia,* and since by this time everybody understood that such weapons were virtually useless against the ironclad, Buchanan was free to use his starboard broadside to hammer away at his target with impunity, unencumbered by any need to protect his own ship. The *Congress* had absorbed tremendous punishment earlier in the battle, when she had been exposed to Confederate guns as the *Virginia* was on her way to the *Cumberland,* and her desultory defense was now weak and brief. A little before 4 P.M., with her commanding officer dead and 135 of her 434 men killed, wounded, or missing, she hauled down her flag in surrender. Most of her surviving crewmen abandoned ship and made for the shore. The battered hulk, already resting on the shallow bottom, angled over with the falling tide.

An exultant Buchanan ordered a cease-fire to let the shallow-draft *Beaufort* and *Raleigh* approach the *Congress* and take off her officers and wounded. It was at this point that something totally unexpected occurred, with significant and unanticipated consequences. The *Virginia* had been exchanging fire with both the U.S. Navy, on board the *Congress*, and the U.S. Army, on shore, and while the navy had surrendered, the army had not. As the crew of the *Raleigh* began transferring the wounded from the *Congress*, the men of the Twentieth Indiana, manning their rifled field pieces at the breastworks at Newport News, began shooting at the Confederate vessels. The fire became so heavy that the victorious Southerners were forced to abandon their efforts and pull away from the *Congress*. Buchanan, who was famous for his excitable nature, became enraged at what he saw as a flagrant violation of the rules of warfare at sea, and ordered his gunners to resume firing on the shore batteries. At the same time, he sent one of his officers back to the *Congress* in a small launch, with orders to burn her. When the army units began targeting the launch, Buchanan rose up in wrath and ordered hot shot and incendiary shells fired into the *Congress*. In the world of wooden warships, hot shot was the single most feared artillery weapon. Solid iron cannonballs were heated in a furnace until they were red-hot, then fired into ships where they started fires that were almost impossible to extinguish. Still livid with anger, Buchanan clambered to the top deck of the *Virginia* and began furiously firing a carbine toward shore. He became an obvious target, and almost immediately, he was hit in the thigh by a sharpshooter's minié ball. While crewmen carried him to his cabin, Lieutenant Jones, his executive officer, took command.

Jones, who had been the first officer assigned to the *Virginia* and probably knew her fighting strengths and weaknesses as intimately as anyone, was impatient to add to the day's glory. He lingered only long enough for the *Virginia*'s gun crews to get the *Congress* well and truly burning before he ordered the ship eastward, toward the grounded and nearly helpless *Minnesota*, lying imprisoned in the mud of the Hampton Roads shallows.

The tide was by this time receding noticeably, and the anxious pilots cautioned Jones that he must keep the *Virginia* well within channels or else she, too, would ground. Limited by her extreme draft, the *Virginia* was forced to stand off over a mile from the *Minnesota*. From that distance, she could inflict only minimum damage, and Jones ordered the remaining hot shot fired into her, only to be told it would not be possible. The only cannon on the *Virginia*'s port side capable of firing hot shot had been knocked out of action by the *Cumberland*'s furious, point-blank fire just before she went down, and it was impossible to transfer either of the two hot shot guns from the starboard battery to bear on the *Minne-*

sota. The simple answer would have been to turn the *Virginia* around and expose her starboard gun ports to the enemy, but such a maneuver would take the best part of an hour, and Lieutenant Jones simply did not have the time. Instead, he sent his two consort gunboats, one to cover the *Minnesota*'s stern and the other her bow, and between them, the three Confederate vessels pummeled the captive frigate until close to 7 P.M., by which time the increasing dark and the rapidly falling tide had forced the *Virginia* to break off the action and retire for the night to an anchorage between Sewell's Point and Craney Island.

It was a remarkable victory for the Confederacy. In a little over four hours of action, the CSS *Virginia* had handed the United States Navy the most humiliating defeat it had ever been forced to endure. It would not suffer a worse one until the Japanese attack at Pearl Harbor, on December 7, 1941.

In a single day, the *Virginia* had totally reversed the strategic balance along the eastern coast of North America, threatened the permanent dislocation of the blockade, and given the South a new and potentially permanent stature among the nations of the world.

11

THE REACTION IN WASHINGTON

The sensational news of the *Virginia*'s awesome debut was carried by telegraph to the most distant parts of the Union and Confederacy. At least two of the telegrams went out through the newly installed underwater cable connecting Fort Monroe to Cape Charles, where the messages were relayed to Washington. The first telegram, written while the battle was still in progress, was sent by General Wool to Edwin Stanton, the secretary of war. It described the loss of the *Cumberland* and *Congress*, and indicated the probability that the *Minnesota* and the *St. Lawrence*, both aground, would be taken the following day. It made no mention of the *Monitor*, which at that time had still not entered Hampton Roads.

A much later message, sent around 10 P.M. by John Worden to Gideon Welles, announced his arrival in Hampton Roads in a succinct and professional manner, but made reference only in the most tangential way to the disastrous state of affairs he found there. "I have the honor to report that I have arrived at this anchorage at nine o'clock this evening and am ordered to proceed immediately to the assistance of the *Minnesota* aground near Newport News."

The *Monitor* had entered Hampton Roads Saturday evening and anchored off the squadron flagship, the *Roanoke*. Worden and Stimers had gone on board to report to Commodore Marston, who filled them in on the grim details of the day's events and predicted that the *Virginia* would undoubtedly reemerge Sunday morning, like Grendel's avenging mother, to finish the job. It was at this meeting that Worden learned for the first time of Gideon Welles's order directing the *Monitor* to bypass Hampton Roads and proceed directly to Washington. That order was still in effect and had indeed been repeated and confirmed in a flood of telegraphed messages to Hampton Roads on both Friday and Saturday. But Marston, as commanding officer, chose to ignore the secretary's order. In light of the significantly altered circumstances brought on by the emergence of the *Virginia* (which almost everyone, Union and Confederate, continued to call the *Merrimac*), Marston proposed to Worden that they disregard the command from Welles and keep the *Monitor* where she was, and assign her to the protection of the *Minnesota*. Worden concurred enthusiastically, and after pausing to send off his message to Welles, he returned to his ship, preparatory to moving her down to where the *Minnesota* lay.

A problem arose when he could not find a pilot to guide the *Monitor* through the treacherous shoals of Hampton Roads. Qualified pilots were loath to volunteer for the job, since anyone who took the assignment would have to remain with the *Monitor* the following day and face the *Virginia* when she once more came out to do battle. Finally, after two hours of searching, Acting Master Samuel Howard volunteered for the pilot's job, and by one in the morning the little ironclad was able to drop down beside the grounded frigate and settle in for the night.

The move coincided with the final, terrible denouement to the day's disaster. The *Congress*, abandoned by her crew and her captors alike, had been burning since late afternoon. (As it turned out, Franklin Buchanan's brother, McKean Buchanan, had survived the afternoon's attack and managed to reach safety.) Throughout the night, the light from the wounded ship's fires had illuminated the Roads from end to end. Now, at last, the wandering flames reached her powder magazine, and with a series of thunderous explosions that could be heard as far as her flames could be seen, the great ship disappeared into smithereens.

As Worden and Stimers labored through the rest of the night to prepare their little craft for the ordeal that was to come, a hundred miles or so up the coast in Washington, the nation's leaders were about to waken to a morning of shock, terror, and despair as the mournful news of the previous day's actions finally reached the nation's capital.

In his diary, Gideon Welles described that Sunday as "that gloomy day, the most so of any I think during the Rebellion." Early that morning, he was leafing through dispatches at his office in the Navy Department, when he was interrupted by an assistant secretary of war, who came hurrying in with a copy of General Wool's telegram to Secretary Stanton describing the awful news of the *Virginia*'s attack. As Welles absorbed the account of the wholesale depredation of the Hampton Roads squadron, he received a summons to the White House, where President Lincoln, in response to the news, had called an emergency meeting of his cabinet.

When Welles arrived at the executive mansion, he found several cabinet members already present, including Secretary of State William Seward, Treasury Secretary Salmon P. Chase, and Stanton. All of them, including Lincoln himself, were in various stages of distress and foreboding. Secretary Stanton was clearly the most frightened man. Lincoln's secretary, John M. Hay, described him as "fearfully stampeded. He said they would capture our fleet, take Ft. Monroe, be in Washington before night." According to Welles, "He could not sit still, or stop to listen to anyone other than himself, and was ready to blame everything on the navy."

Stanton kept jumping up and looking out the window, which gave onto a superb view of the Potomac, as if expecting to see the *Virginia* steaming up at any moment. Lincoln asked Welles what could be done to stop her if she did come up to Washington. "I told the President she could not, if in the river, with her heavy armor, cross the Kettle Bottom Shoals." This was a relief to almost everyone in the room. "Mr. Seward, who had been desponding, contrary to his usual temperament and custom, rendered more timid by the opinion and alarm of Stanton, said my remark in relation to the draft of water of the *Merrimac* gave him the first moment's relief he had experienced."

Stanton alone refused to be comforted.

As the frightened cabinet officers attempted to get a clearer picture of the situation, an even more daunting possibility occurred to Stanton, and he warned that the Confederate ironclad "might go to New York and Boston and destroy those cities, or levy from them contributions sufficient to carry on the War."

Welles pointed out reasonably enough that she could not come to Washington and go to New York at the same time, and when Stanton demanded to know what vessel or means the Union had to resist or prevent her from doing whatever she pleased, Welles replied that the *Monitor* was now in Hampton Roads, and that he had confidence in her power to resist, and, if all went well, to overcome, the Southern monster.

Stanton made "some sneering inquiry about this new vessel the *Monitor*, of which he admitted he knew little or nothing." Welles described the ship briefly. Stanton then asked about her armament, and when Welles told him, "his mingled look of incredulity and contempt cannot be described; and the tone of his voice, as he asked if my reliance was on that craft with her two guns, is equally indescribable."

When the meeting broke up, Stanton hurried off to send frantic telegraphic messages to governors of all Northern states bordering the Atlantic, and to the mayors of the major seaports along the coast, alerting them to the imminent danger he foresaw, and advising them how best to face the terrifying prospect of attack by an invincible ironclad.

Welles, who had a grudging respect for Stanton but did not like him, can be forgiven for casting an almost comic light on the events in Washington on March 9, 1862. He found "something inexpressibly ludicrous in the wild, frantic talk, action, and rage of Stanton as he ran from room to room, sat down and jumped up after writing a few words, swung his arms, scolded, and raved." But Welles also admits "that day and its incidents were among the most unpleasant and uncomfortable of my life. The events were momentous and portentous to the nation, the responsibility and the consequence of the disaster were heavier on me than on any other individual." Subsequent events were to make Stanton's actions seem little short of ridiculous, but it would be a long time before even Welles was to learn all the particulars in the case, and know enough to make a realistic appraisal of the threat represented by the *Virginia*.

Probably the most reasonable assessment of that famous meeting in the White House relates not to Stanton's childish outbursts but to the fact that the depredations of the *Virginia* had made every one of the leaders in Washington, including Lincoln and Welles, acutely aware of the importance of Hampton Roads, and by extension, the importance of the *Monitor*, and given her a unique significance even before she was ever tested in battle. It is fair to say that the worshipful, almost mythic aura that would soon surround the *Monitor* had its beginnings in that impromptu cabinet meeting.

12

THE BATTLE

The red, clear dawn that broke over Hampton Roads on March 9, 1862, promised another seasonably beautiful day, but as always in the Roads, it was not the weather that would govern the activities so much as it was the tides. The movement of water in and out of Chesapeake Bay, the currents generated by that movement, and the channels cleared by those currents, dictated where and when a ship might best go about it, all of which would be vital factors in the battle to come.

Off Sewell's Point, where the *Virginia* lay at anchor surrounded by her little band of gunboat consorts, Lieutenant Jones was eager to get under way as early as possible and finish the work he and his crew had so spectacularly initiated the day before. Flag Officer Buchanan's wound had worsened during the night, and it had been necessary to send him off to the hospital, so Jones was still in command of the ship. In one of his last acts before retiring, Jones had ordered the cooks to prepare a heroes' meal for the men who had so gallantly earned it the previous day. And to make sure they had time to enjoy it, he ordered the boatswain to awaken them before dawn. As one crewman later recalled with satisfaction, "We began the day with two jiggers of whiskey and a hearty breakfast."

Standing on the promenade deck of his ship at first light, Jones could see, some four miles to the north, the last remnants of the *Congress*, reduced now to a shapeless lump, still fitfully burning, her masts and rigging long since gone, and only portions of her hulk remaining. A couple of points to the east, illuminated by the fires from the *Congress*, sat the great bulk of the *Minnesota*, still imprisoned in the shallows. Beyond her, toward Fort Monroe, lay the *St. Lawrence*, equally helpless in her grounded state. Both warships, waiting meekly like sacrificial lambs, would be easy prey for the invincible *Virginia*. Their destruction, and with it the unraveling of the entire Union blockade, appeared at that moment preordained.

There was a tugboat near the *Minnesota*, and according to some accounts, another nondescript vessel, a low, raftlike thing with what appeared to be a large water tank on her deck. In the early-morning light it was difficult to guess what she might be, and since the officers and men of the *Virginia* were concerned with more pressing matters, they had neither the interest nor the inclination to ponder the significance of the unknown vessel.

Breakfast on board the *Monitor* that morning

was a somewhat less jolly affair than the feast being served up on board the *Virginia*. Many of the *Monitor*'s weary crew had not slept for over forty-eight hours and were so exhausted they moved about the vessel in a daze, munching absently on cold biscuit, the only food available from the galley.

Lack of sleep was the most serious problem, but there were other vexations that were almost equally disagreeable. The men, after having heroically saved their ship from foundering twice in thirty-six hours, now found themselves the targets of wisecracks, derided as fools bent upon a fool's errand. A civilian tugboat captain, who had been summoned to the grounded *Minnesota* during the night for a last, futile attempt to get her off the shoals, sized up the *Monitor* by the dim light of the half-moon and dismissed her with a shrug. "What can that little thing do?" he asked with a sardonic laugh. "We could lick her ourselves." Like thousands of others, he had witnessed the *Virginia* in action and could not imagine how the little *Monitor*, barely half her size, could possibly stand up to the awesome destructive power of the Confederate ironclad.

At dawn, Lieutenant Worden and his officers clambered to the top of the *Monitor*'s turret and trained their glasses to the south, to get their first glimpse of the *Virginia*. Smoke was already rising from her stack, and Worden gave orders to notify him as soon as there was any sign that she was about to get under way. He did not have long to wait. Around 7:30 A.M., the *Virginia* was seen to slip her moorings and, accompanied by the *Patrick Henry*, the *Jamestown*, and the *Teaser*, steam out into the main channel, heading in the direction of Fort Monroe. Once in the open, the little flotilla veered to port and stood directly for the *Minnesota*.

As the Confederates drew closer to their target, they could make out the strange-looking craft, which had effectually been concealed by the immense bulk of the *Minnesota*, moving away from the side of the steam frigate. The executive officer of the *Patrick Henry* described it as "such a craft as the eyes of a seaman never looked upon before — an immense shingle floating in the water, with a gigantic cheese box rising from its center; no sails, no wheels, no smokestack, no guns. What could it be?" The lack of a smokestack implied that whatever else she was, the vessel had no engine. Midshipman Littlepage of the *Virginia* thought it might be a raft carrying one of the *Minnesota*'s boilers in for repairs. Lieutenant J. R. Eggleston, a gunnery officer on board the *Virginia*, called her "the strangest looking craft we had ever seen before."

Lieutenant Jones, who for several months had been closely following the reports on the *Monitor*'s construction that appeared regularly in the Northern newspapers, knew at once what the strange ship was, but chose to ignore her for the present. He was determined to finish off the *Min-*

nesota before he turned his attention to the new ironclad. When he was still about a mile from the stranded frigate, he gave the order to commence firing, and almost immediately, the *Virginia*'s forward seven-inch rifle scored a hit that quickly started a fire. At virtually the same moment, the stern gun of the *Minnesota* returned fire, with a shot that ricocheted harmlessly off the *Virginia*'s armor, and the battle commenced.

On board the *Monitor*, two officers, Acting Assistant Paymaster William F. Keeler and Surgeon D. C. Logue, were standing on the turret when the first shell from the *Virginia* whistled overhead. Captain Worden turned to them and said calmly but sternly, "Gentlemen, that is the *Merrimac*, you had better go below." Without another word, the three men scurried down the hatch.

Worden quickly made his way to the bow and took his place in the pilothouse, crowded into the confined space with the pilot and the ship's quartermaster. Peering out through the narrow slit that served as the only means of observation in the entire ship, he ordered the quartermaster to steer for the shallow waters midway between the oncoming *Virginia* and the stationary *Minnesota*. His orders were to protect the *Minnesota*, and he meant to do just that.

Captain Van Brunt, standing on the quarterdeck of the *Minnesota*, watched with amazement as Worden deliberately placed his little ship in harm's way. Later, in his official report, he described how the *Monitor* had steamed directly at the *Virginia*, and how, "much to my astonishment, laid herself right alongside of the *Merrimac*, and the contrast was that of a pygmy to a giant."

As Worden approached the Confederate flotilla, the wooden vessels escorting the *Virginia* dispersed quickly, and the two ironclads found themselves alone in the north channel of the Roads, a pair of heavily clad armored knights met upon a watery field of honor. As soon as Worden came within short range of the *Virginia*, he changed his course so as to come alongside of her, stopped his engines, and gave the order to commence firing. Lieutenant Greene, the executive officer in the turret, triced up a port, ran out a gun, and taking deliberate aim, pulled the lockstring, and the eleven-inch Dahlgren erupted. On the *Virginia*, Midshipman Littlepage, still under the impression that the *Monitor* was a barge carrying one of the *Minnesota*'s boilers, thought the boiler had exploded when he saw the gun smoke, but was quickly disabused of his error when a 180-pound projectile slammed into the *Virginia*, glancing off the casement's angled shield. The Confederate ship answered almost immediately with a rattling broadside from her own battery, making the *Monitor*'s turret ring like a mad, cacophonous bell as shot after shot hit home. But for all the deafening clamor inside the revolving drum, there was no damage, and all the men crowded into the turret — sixteen gunners and three officers — suddenly grasped in a dazzling rush of revelation that their ship was impregnable, and that they could not be harmed by any gun in Hampton Roads.

Both vessels then turned and passed each other again, and for the first time it was possible to gauge the significant technical differences between the two ships. For all her ironcladding, the *Virginia* was still a very traditionally designed vessel, a floating gun platform built around her broadside battery. She could bring her main guns into action only by exposing the entire side of the ship. In effect it was the helmsman at the wheel who actually aimed the cannon, while the gunners simply loaded and fired them. In contrast, the *Monitor*'s design made the positioning of the ship almost irrelevant to the aiming of the guns. It was the men who controlled the turret — the same men in charge of working and fighting the guns — who did the aiming and firing.

The fight continued at very short range, with the exchange of broadsides as fast as the guns could be served. The distance between the vessels was frequently no more than a few yards. Worden took full advantage of the fact that he had the far more maneuverable vessel, and kept trying to find some vulnerable spot to attack in his adversary. At one point he made a dash at her stern, hoping to disable her screw, but the move required precise aim, and he missed by a foot or two.

As the battle progressed, it became obvious to

the men in the *Monitor* that there were some serious drawbacks in Ericsson's revolutionary design. One of the first problems to manifest itself concerned the communications link between the two most vital areas of the ship, the pilothouse and the gun turret. Early in the action the speaking tube link broke down, and two of the ship's officers, Lieutenant Keeler and the captain's clerk, Daniel Toffey, were assigned to run back and forth between the pilothouse and the turret to relay orders from the captain. As Lieutenant Greene, in the turret, described it, "The situation was novel: a vessel of war was engaged in desperate combat with a powerful foe, the captain, commanding and guiding, was enclosed in one place, and the executive officer, working and fighting the guns, was shut up in another." Greene was quick to praise Keeler and Toffey for their zeal and alacrity, "but both being landsmen, our technical communications sometimes miscarried."

Nor was the working of the turret altogether satisfactory. Greene found it difficult to get it started revolving, and once started, found it equally difficult to stop. "The conditions were very different from those of an ordinary broadside gun under which we had been trained on wooden ships," Greene wrote. "My only view of the world outside . . . was over the muzzles of the guns, which cleared the ports by only a few inches. When the guns were run in, the portholes were covered by heavy iron pendulums. . . . To hoist these pendulums required the entire gun's crew and vastly increased the work inside the turret."

It also became impossible to maintain any bearings inside the turret. White marks had been placed upon the stationary deck immediately below the turret to indicate the direction of the starboard and port sides, as well as the bow and stern, but these marks were obliterated early in the action, and the men in the turret lost all sense of orientation.

Perhaps the most serious of the problems concerned the rotation of the turret. Although it could in theory turn and fire in any direction, in practice Greene discovered that he could not fire directly ahead, nor within several points of the bow, since, in his opinion, the blast from the guns would have injured the people in the pilothouse. Nor could he fire directly astern, for fear of concussion rupturing her boilers.

Eventually Lieutenant Greene and his men worked out a makeshift system for controlling the turret that worked with tolerable effectiveness. The awkward iron pendulums that were designed to cover the ports were left permanently open, so as to give the men a freer hand for swabbing out and reloading the guns. During the seven or eight minutes it took to reload, the turret was turned away from the enemy, so as to protect the gun crews. When a gun was once again ready for firing, it was run out the porthole, and the turret was set in motion. Greene, with his hand on the firing lanyard and his eye on the changing scene as seen through the porthole, would search for a target, and when it came into view, he would jerk the lanyard "on the fly" and let the turret continue turning until it again faced away from the enemy. It was a tricky maneuver, requiring delicate timing and a constant awareness of the dangers involved in firing too close to the pilothouse. For this and other reasons, Greene arranged to fire every shot that day, until subsequent developments took him away from the turret.

A little after 10 A.M., the pilots on board the *Virginia*, possibly confused by the heat of the action, ran the ship aground on the shoals. She was unable to move, and the *Monitor*, which could move freely in virtually any direction because of her shallow draft, began circling the enemy like a pit bull, searching for some weak point.

The *Virginia*'s engineering officer, H. Ashton Ramsay, instantly recognized the full extent of the peril. "Our situation was critical," he would write later. The ship had used up so much coal in the two days of fighting that she now rode high out of the water, exposing her unprotected underside, and the *Monitor* "might have pierced us between wind and water had she depressed her guns." Ramsay did everything he could think of to free the ship from her muddy prison. "We lashed down the safety valves, heaped quick-burning combustibles into the already raging fires, and brought the boilers to a pressure that would have been unsafe under ordinary circumstances."

At one point, while the *Virginia* was still immobilized, Lieutenant Jones hurried down from the spar deck and saw the crews standing idly by their guns. He turned angrily to the officer in charge and demanded, "Why are you not firing, Mr. Eggleston?"

"Why, our powder is very precious," Eggleston replied, "and after two hours' incessant firing I find I can do her about as much damage by snapping my thumb at her every two minutes and a half."

For agonizing minutes, Ramsay's efforts to free the ship continued to fail. "The propeller churned the mud and water furiously," he wrote, "but the ship did not stir. We piled on oiled cotton waste, splints of wood, anything that would burn faster than coal. It seemed impossible that the boilers could stand the pressure we were crowding upon them." At last, "there was a perceptible movement, and the *Merrimack* [sic] slowly dragged herself off the shoal by main strength."

Jones, seeing that the *Virginia*'s guns could not hurt the *Monitor*, decided to ram her. Even without her iron ram, he reasoned, the great weight of his ship would be enough to drive the smaller one under. He explained his plan to his officers and announced that after running her down, he would board her. While his officers organized a boarding party and worked out a plan for overrunning the *Monitor*'s turret, Jones tried to get his vessel into position. "The ship was as unwieldy as Noah's ark," according to one of her junior officers, Lieutenant John Taylor Wood. After almost an hour of painfully slow and clumsy maneuvering, Jones finally saw an opportunity and ordered, "Go ahead, full steam!" But before the *Virginia* could gather headway, the *Monitor* had turned nimbly aside, and the *Virginia* barely grazed her. At the moment of collision Lieutenant Greene, in the turret, planted a solid 180-pound shot fair and square upon the forward part of the *Virginia*'s casement. As Greene observed ruefully, "Had the gun been loaded with thirty pounds of powder, which was the charge subsequently used with similar guns, it is probable that this shot would have penetrated her armor; but the charge being limited to fifteen pounds, in accordance with peremptory orders to that effect from the Navy Department, the shot rebounded without doing any more damage than possibly to start some of the beams of her armor-backing."

One of the many ironies of the battle was the strict limitation imposed on the amount of gunpowder that could be used in the *Monitor*'s cannon. The limitations had been instituted by the U.S. Navy many years earlier as a direct result of the 1843 explosion aboard the *Princeton*, the disaster that had been unfairly blamed on Ericsson. Now, almost twenty years later, another Ericsson warship was still paying for the navy's old blunders.

The *Monitor* turned again and came up on the Confederates' after quarter, her bow actually touching, and this time Greene fired both of her guns at point-blank range. The two shots struck about halfway up the shield, abreast of the after pivot gun, and the impact forced in the side two or three inches. The crews of the *Virginia*'s after guns were knocked over by the terrific concussion and left stunned and bleeding at the nose, mouth, and ears. One of the officers on board the *Virginia* wrote later that another shot at the same point would undoubtedly have penetrated his ship's otherwise impregnable shield.

The boarding party huddled on the forward deck was called away, but before anyone could clamber on board the *Monitor*, she had slipped off.

After three hours of bombardment, the supply of shot in the *Monitor*'s turret was exhausted, and Worden hauled off into shallow waters to replenish his stock of cannonballs from the storage bins on the berth deck. The hoisting of the heavy shot was a slow and tedious operation, since access to the turret was through two scuttles, one in the deck and the other in the floor of the turret, and in order for them to be aligned, the turret had to remain stationary. Worden took advantage of the lull to climb through the porthole onto the deck to make a quick examination of any damage to his ship.

The *Virginia*, unable to follow the *Monitor* into shallow waters, once again turned her attention to attacking the *Minnesota*. Captain Van Brunt ordered the gunners of the *Minnesota* to fire at will, and the entire port battery, plus the ship's powerful ten-inch pivot gun, erupted in angry defiance. It was a broadside "which would have blown out of the water any timber-built ship in the world," the captain recalled later, but it had absolutely no effect upon the *Virginia*, which continued firing unabated.

As soon as the *Monitor*'s guns were resupplied, she returned to the fight, and it was at this point that Worden's luck ran out. A shell from one of the *Virginia*'s guns, fired when the muzzle was not ten yards distant, made a direct hit on the forward side of the pilothouse and exploded on impact. At that moment Worden had his face pressed against the inner bulkhead of the pilothouse, trying to follow the action through the viewing slit in the iron shield, and he took the full force of the explosion, which momentarily stunned and utterly blinded him. The explosion tore away some of the wrought iron that shielded the pilothouse and flooded it with daylight. Worden, blind as he was, could sense the bright light and the cool air, and concluded that the pilothouse was seriously damaged, if not destroyed. He gave orders to put the helm to starboard and sheer off. The men in the *Virginia*, who were unaware of the effect of their salvo, saw the *Monitor* retire once again to the shallow middle ground of the Roads and interpreted the move as a withdrawal from the fight, when in fact it was simply a measure designed to give the *Monitor* a chance to assess damages.

Worden summoned Greene from the turret, and the executive officer hurried forward to find his captain standing at the foot of the ladder to the pilothouse, holding on to it for dear life. "He was a ghastly sight," Greene recalled, "with his eyes closed and the blood apparently rushing from every pore in the upper part of his face. He told me he was seriously wounded and directed me to take command. I assisted in leading him to a sofa in his cabin, where he was tenderly cared for by Dr. Logue, and then I assumed command."

Greene hurried forward to the pilothouse, quickly ascertained that the damage was less than had at first been feared, and gave the order to return to the fight. About twenty minutes had elapsed since the *Monitor*'s withdrawal, and by this time the *Virginia*, which was having trouble with her engines and was leaking from the pounding she had received the day before in her battle with the *Cumberland*, had already turned away from the scene of action. Greene and the others in the pilothouse, making a mistake similar to that of the Southerners, interpreted the *Virginia*'s move as a retreat. He shouted out the good news, and the entire *Monitor* erupted with a mighty cheer of triumph. The men in the turret managed to get off another shot or two at the retreating *Virginia*, and then Greene ordered the helmsman to turn away and proceed toward the stranded *Minnesota*.

The blinded Worden, lying helpless in his cabin, asked weakly for news of the battle. When told that the *Minnesota* had been saved, he lay back on his pillow and said, "Then I can die happy."

It was around 12:30 P.M. when the *Monitor* bore up to the *Minnesota* and let go her anchor. The assistant secretary of the navy, Gustavus Fox, who had witnessed the entire action, came on board to congratulate the crew and to join the officers for a lunch of beef steak and green peas in the wardroom. "Well, gentlemen," he said cheerfully, "you don't look as though you were just through one of the greatest naval conflicts on record." "No sir," Lieutenant Greene answered cockily, "we haven't done much fighting, merely drilling the men at the guns a little."

By the end of the day, Lieutenant Greene's bluff bravado had given way to exhaustion, as he described in a private letter home. "I had been up so long, and been under such a state of excitement, that my nervous system was completely run down. . . . My nerves and muscles twitched as though electric shocks were continually passing through them. . . . I laid down and tried to sleep — I might as well have tried to fly."

13

AFTERMATH

What are we to make of this first great clash of ironclads? It was by any definition a strange and extraordinary battle: two untested, experimental ships, knocked together at breakneck speed, and each manned by an inexperienced crew, caught up in a do-or-die contest in front of an audience of twenty thousand cheering spectators crowded together like fans at a football game. For all the weight of metal hurled that day, there were no fatalities on board either ship and only a handful of wounded. All this in a battle of such strategic significance that it has been ranked with Gettysburg in its importance to the Civil War.

Which ship was the victor, and which the vanquished? The answer depended entirely on who asked the question. As Lieutenant S. Dana Greene of the *Monitor* stated ruefully in a comment published twenty-five years after the battle, "We . . . thought, and still think, that we had gained a great victory. This the Confederates have denied."

At almost the same time that the assistant secretary of the navy was congratulating the men of the *Monitor*, throngs of cheering partisans were lining the banks of the Elizabeth to welcome the *Virginia* as she made her way upriver to Norfolk. A beaming Lieutenant Jones ordered his officers to the promenade deck to accept the plaudits of the crowd, while small boats filled with spectators jammed the river and formed a victory procession all the way to the navy yard. After a brief speech of thanks by Jones, the crew went into town, where the partying and celebration continued long into the night.

The ailing Buchanan, convalescing at the naval hospital, dictated a letter to Mallory containing the details of the two days' action, with major emphasis on the glorious triumphs of the first day, and sent it off to Richmond by train with one of his officers, along with a traditional symbol of victory, the rolled-up flag of the *Congress*. When the officer reached the capital, Stephen Mallory immediately escorted him to a meeting with President Davis and several cabinet members, so that they might hear the story of the *Virginia*'s triumphs firsthand. After providing a detailed account of the action, the officer dramatically unfurled the captured flag, only to discover that it was saturated with blood. The grizzly sight put a momentary damper on the celebration. Every man in the room had at one time or another sworn allegiance to the same flag. It was quickly rolled up again and sent to Mallory's office for safekeeping, and has never been seen since.

One of those present at the meeting was Judah

P. Benjamin, the Confederate secretary of war who was soon to become Davis's secretary of state. Looking ahead to his new post, he recognized that the *Virginia*'s exploits could be used as a powerful weapon of propaganda, and an important means of persuading the powers in London and Paris to extend diplomatic recognition to the Confederacy. He proclaimed that the *Virginia*'s success "evinces our ability to break the much-vaunted blockade, and ere the lapse of ninety days we hope to drive from our waters the whole blockading fleet."

Back in Norfolk, the yard constructor counted ninety-seven indentations in the *Virginia*'s armor from shot, twenty of which could be definitely ascribed to the *Monitor*'s Dahlgrens, and most of the rest to army batteries at Newport News and guns on the other vessels she had fought during her two days in the Roads. Six of her top layers of plate had been broken by the *Monitor*'s guns. She was returned to dry dock for repairs and modifications, and so eager was everyone to get her back in action that the yard instituted an around-the-clock schedule of work. An additional covering of two-inch iron plate was added to the hull, so that the *Virginia*'s armor now reached four feet below the shield. A new and heavier ram was secured to her bow, a twelve-foot-long steel monster designed to reach beneath the *Monitor*'s overhanging deck. Two new guns replaced those damaged in the fighting, and the wrought-iron port shutters that Buchanan had left behind on the dock in his eagerness to get into action were finally fixed in place.

Along with the improvements in her armor, the *Virginia* would also carry a new and more deadly sting. The Tredegar works sent down lethal new projectiles for her seven-inch rifles, made of steel and wrought iron and designed to penetrate the *Monitor*'s armored turret at a range of one hundred yards. The Confederate ironclad would be a far more formidable opponent when next the two vessels met.

In Washington, the response to the news from Hampton Roads was every bit as enthusiastic as it was in Richmond. The widespread fear of the *Virginia*, characterized by Edwin Stanton's hysteria in the White House early on Sunday, gave way to an almost giddy sense of excitement and relief. The day after the battle, Gideon Welles escorted an eyewitness, Lieutenant Henry A. Wise, over to the White House to give Lincoln a blow-by-blow account of the events. The president was greatly moved by the description of Lieutenant Worden's wounds, and on learning that Worden was a personal friend of Wise, and that he was in Washington recuperating at Wise's home, Lincoln asked to meet the hero. The house was nearby, and the two men proceeded on foot. On entering Worden's second-story room, Wise said, "Jack, here's the President, who has come to see you." Worden, lying in bed with his head swathed in bandages, groped for Lincoln's proffered hand and said, "You do me a great honor, Mr. President, and I am only sorry that I can't see you."

Lincoln answered solemnly, "You have done me more honor, sir, than I can ever do to you." Then he sat on the edge of the bed and asked Worden to tell him the story of the battle all over again.

Worden's account differed in at least one respect from the version Lincoln had heard from Welles and Wise. Worden told the president that while he found much to praise in the *Monitor*, which was indeed shot- and shell-proof, during the course of the battle he had come to realize how vulnerable she was to another form of attack, namely boarding. While the ship's heavy armor and lack of ports made it difficult for attackers to enter the *Monitor*, the same conditions made it equally difficult for members of the crew to prevent anyone from climbing on deck. Once on board, boarders could easily stop the turret from rotating and then create chaos by dousing the fires through the exhausts and tossing a few hand grenades into the turret's gun ports. The danger of boarders could be dealt with, Worden told Lincoln, so long as the ship had enough sea room in which to maneuver, but if she was in any way restricted in her ability to take evasive action, her vulnerability would be serious.

Lincoln thanked Worden, and as he made his good-byes, promised the lieutenant that if it lay within his powers to do so, he would see that he was promoted to captain. Immediately on his return to the White House, Lincoln sent a message to Welles, relaying Worden's warning. "I have just seen Lieut. Worden, who says the 'Monitor' could be boarded and captured very easily — first, after boarding, by wedging the turret, so that it would not turn, and then by pouring water in her & drowning her machinery. He is decidedly of the opinion she should not go sky-larking up to Norfolk."

Later that day, in response to Lincoln's expressed fears, Welles sent a telegram to the naval commander at Hampton Roads: "It is directed by the President that the *Monitor* be not too much exposed; that under no event shall any attempt be made to proceed with her unattended to Norfolk."

Over the next two months, the *Virginia* made three more sorties down the Elizabeth to challenge the *Monitor* for a return engagement, but in each case, the Union ship, under express orders not to fight unless the *Virginia* ventured out of Hampton Roads, refused to take the bait. The Confederates were disdainful of what they perceived as rank cowardice, and when, on May 8, at the last encounter of the two ironclads, the *Monitor* again took cover under the protection of the guns at Fort Monroe, the captain of the *Virginia* ordered his men to fire a single gun to windward, the ultimate naval expression of contempt.

The *Virginia*'s insult was mortifying to the men of the *Monitor*. By that date they had become accustomed to being lionized in the press and hailed as the saviors of national honor. Two months of adulation had convinced them they were the fiercest, most gallant warriors in the navy, and it galled them mightily that their superiors would not allow them to take up the rebel's challenge. But for all the bravado and hurt feelings of the crew, the caution of their superiors made good sense. Unless she made a threatening move, there was no longer any reason to fight the *Virginia*, and to do so would only have been a foolish waste of resources.

The North and South had assessed the same two-day battle and come up with radically different interpretations. The exuberant crowds that had gathered on the banks of the Elizabeth to cheer the perceived victory of the *Virginia* were taking a naive measure of events. On Saturday the *Virginia* had destroyed two Union warships, and on Sunday she had fought the *Monitor* to a standstill, with neither ship a clear winner. Making the same mistake common to novice chess players when they measure their success on the board in terms of the number of pieces they capture, the Southerners reckoned their ship had done spectacularly well the first day (which was true), and since she had done at least as well as the Yankees on the second (which, in a very narrow sense, was also true), she could be seen as the overall victor.

But as any experienced chess player knows, success has nothing to do with kill rates. The only point of the game is checkmating the king. Whatever other mayhem one player manages to inflict upon an opponent's pieces is irrelevant. The same, of course, is true of war.

The North understood this better than the South. To Yankee eyes, an analysis of the same two days' action appeared quite different. The first day's action was clearly an unequivocal Southern victory, which seriously threatened to punch a permanent hole in the blockade, and thereby usher in European recognition of the Confederacy with all its attendant problems for the North. But the arrival of the *Monitor*, and her subsequent standoff with the *Virginia*, proved to the world that the *Virginia* was not strong enough to break the blockade. In that single, seemingly equivocal four-hour action on March 9, the Confederacy lost its last real opportunity for European intervention, and with it, the war.

In a bizarre postscript to the battle, it was eventually confirmed that the United States Navy did not even fully own the *Monitor* at the time of the action. It was not until March 14, 1862, almost a week after the battle, that the builders of the ironclad received their final payment in the amount of $68,750.

On the same day, John Winslow had good news for his silent partner, Congressman Erastus Corning: Their investment was about to pay off in spectacular fashion. "We have closed for 6 boats on the plan of the *Monitor* for $400,000 each — they are to be a trifle larger in size — this will do."

What had a few months earlier been "Ericsson's Folly," a one-off ironclad specifically built to hold Hampton Roads, had been transformed into an entire class of naval vessels, the first of several different classes of monitors that would dominate the American navy for the rest of the war and years beyond. Of the forty ironclads laid down by the Union during the war, thirty-five would be monitors. Some of them were formidable indeed. The *Kalamazoo*, designed for ocean sailing, had twin turrets, fore and aft, each one armed with a pair of fifteen-inch Dahlgrens. Still more monitors were built after the war. The design had a remarkable longevity, and monitors were still being used for coastal defense well into the 1920s. The last one, the USS *Cheyenne*, was not stricken from the Navy List until 1937.

14

THE END OF THE *MONITOR*

The *Virginia*'s defiant gunshot to windward at her final meeting with the *Monitor* turned out to be her last offensive action. Two days later, on May 10, when the Confederate army moved north to defend Richmond, rebel troops were forced to abandon Norfolk, thus depriving the *Virginia* of a home port. Her crew tried vainly to lighten her draft enough to get her up the James River so that she could help defend Richmond. When that failed, they had no alternative except to destroy her to keep her out of Yankee hands. Her captain ran her aground at Craney Island, then ordered her set afire before marching her crew twenty-two miles to Suffolk, where they all took the train to Richmond. Around 5 A.M. on May 11, two months and two days after her encounter with the *Monitor*, the flames reached the *Virginia*'s magazine and she blew up.

The *Monitor*, now deprived of her reason for being, remained in Hampton Roads throughout the summer of 1862, save for a single sortie up the James to support McClellan's army attack. She and a few other Union vessels got as far as

Drewry's Bluff, below Richmond, where they were stopped by Confederate guns commanding the river. By a turn of fate that has often been remarked upon, the rebel guns at Drewry's Bluff were manned by members of the *Virginia*'s crew, and the flag that flew over their battery was that of their old ship. In the ensuing exchange of fire the Southern guns were again unable to penetrate the *Monitor*'s armor, but the men in the turret were unable to elevate her guns high enough to return the fire from the bluff, and eventually the *Monitor* was forced to withdraw ignominiously downriver, having accomplished nothing.

On her return to the Roads, she lay at anchor throughout the summer, where her men were forced to live aboard an increasingly uncomfortable ship, which, as they discovered to their dismay, held the sun's heat like a saucepan. The interior temperature aboard ship often reached 140 degrees during the day and was only marginally cooler at night. The new captain, William N. Jeffers, did not help the situation. He was a cold, precise man, an ordnance expert who disliked the ship and continually complained about her. Keeler noted that he "lacked that noble kindness of heart & quiet unassuming manner to both officers & men which endeared Capt. Worden to all on board." Jeffers had been in command at the Drewry's Bluff fiasco, and upon their return to Hampton Roads, he and Lieutenant Greene, who remained as the ship's executive officer, drew up a list of complaints about the design and construction of the *Monitor*.

Their report was generally dismissive and at times even contemptuous of the ship. It stated that her battle with the *Virginia* "caused an exaggerated confidence to be entertained by the public in the powers of the *Monitor*." The generally disparaging analysis, which was submitted on May 22, 1862, complained of the poor visibility from the pilothouse and suggested that it be moved to the top of the turret, which would give the captain a superior vantage point and protect him and the helmsman from all but the heaviest seas. The report was particularly critical of the turret's traversing capabilities, asserting that "the guns cannot be fired nearer to the line of the keel than 30 degrees when underway without deafening the persons in the pilot house." It was even more critical of the ship's ability to fire toward the stern, stating that "it would be highly imprudent to fire aft at a greater angle than 50 degrees. The effect of firing over the boilers is very great, and several successive fires would undoubtedly set them leaking, if nothing worse happened." In short, the report claimed that rather than the virtual 360-degree traverse claimed by her builders, the *Monitor*'s turret could fire only about 100 degrees to either side, which would represent a more restricted range of fire than the *Virginia*'s.

Jeffers also complained of the ship's rate of fire. "Her military force is greatly diminished by inability to fire, or rather to run out, both guns at once. The time lost in raising the pendulum and running out the second gun often loses the favorable position, besides giving the enemy better opportunities for getting shot into the ports."

There was a long list of additional complaints covering the engine room, the galley, and the crew's quarters. In summing up, Jeffers concluded, "For general purposes wooden ships . . . have not yet been superseded."

For John Ericsson, who had suffered for almost twenty years from the carping and backbiting of naval brass, Jeffers's complaints were simply further proof, if such was necessary, that the navy had no idea how to operate his ship. Directly addressing the problem that both Greene and Jeffers had raised relating to aiming to either side of the pilothouse, Ericsson claimed the pilothouse obstructed forward aiming only six degrees to either side of the keel line, not the thirty degrees they claimed. He insisted that it was "a structure too substantial to suffer from the mere aerial current produced by the flight of the shot."

On the question of the heavy port stoppers that required so much time and effort to open and close, Ericsson peevishly pointed out that in combat conditions, the stoppers were not designed to be opened and closed with each shot, but to be left open, and the gun crews would be protected by having the entire turret turn away from enemy fire, a simple operation requiring one man using only one hand on the appropriate lever. During the battle with the *Virginia*, Lieutenant Greene had hit upon precisely the same idea of turning the turret to protect the men inside, not realizing that such was the original intention of the inventor.

As for moving the pilothouse to the top of the turret, a suggestion that had been made many times, Ericsson labeled the idea "obvious" and said that it had been "carefully considered before the *Monitor* turret was constructed," and that the idea was rejected only because it would have delayed completion of the ship for a month or more. "The damage to the national course which might have resulted from that delay is beyond computation," he concluded icily.

By the end of summer, marine fouling of the *Monitor*'s bottom had grown so thick as to reduce her speed to two or three knots, and finally, in September, she was ordered to Washington Navy Yard for an overhaul. The crew was rewarded with shore leave, and the ship became the city's most popular tourist attraction, drawing notables from the president on down, and on at least one occasion a fashionable crowd of Washington ladies who proved zealous souvenir hunters. "When we came up to clean that night, there was not a key, doorknob, escutcheon — there wasn't a thing that hadn't been carried away," one officer recorded.

By November, a clean, scraped *Monitor* was back at Hampton Roads, and the men settled once again into the boring duty of guarding what was now a backwater of the war.

On Christmas Day, they received orders to proceed to Beaufort, North Carolina, to assist in the blockade of Wilmington, on the Cape Fear River. Not everyone was enthused by the prospect. Lieutenant Greene, one of the few men left on board who had experienced the *Monitor*'s harrowing trip from New York the previous March, was appalled at the prospect. "I do not consider this steamer a seagoing vessel," he warned. "She has not the steam power to go against a head wind or sea, and . . . would not steer even in smooth weather, and going slow she does not mind her helm readily." Everyone agreed with Greene's assessment, but it was hoped that they could avoid the problems of her maiden voyage by having her towed, not by a small tug like the *Seth Low*, but by the large, recently built steamer *Rhode Island*, a powerful, 236-foot-long sidewheeler.

But if the navy was prepared to provide a better tow, it was not prepared to change the way it readied the *Monitor* for her voyage around Cape Hatteras, a coastline notorious for the most treacherous weather on the entire eastern seaboard of North America.

"The turret and sightholes were caulked," recalled Dr. Grenville Weeks, the ship's surgeon, "and every possible entrance for water made secure, only the smallest opening being left in the turret top." The navy was once again deliberately ignoring the fact that Ericsson had specifically designed the *Monitor*'s turret to fit snugly into a watertight brass ring set into the deck, and that no packing was necessary. The new captain of the *Monitor*, John Bankhead, precisely duplicated the same ill-conceived precaution that had come close to sinking the *Monitor* off the New Jersey coast.

At 2:30 P.M. on December 29, with the weather "clear and pleasant, and every prospect of its continuation," the *Rhode Island* took up the tow, consisting of two very stout hawsers, one of eleven inches circumference, and the other of fifteen inches, and set off toward the Virginia Capes. The *Monitor* and *Rhode Island* were accompanied by the steamer *State of Georgia* and one of John Ericsson's new ironclad monitors (the name was already generic), the *Passaic*. The wind was light and out of the southwest as they made Cape Henry and plunged into the winter Atlantic, turning south to the Carolinas.

The first night passed without incident, but by noon the following day the wind had freshened, and the *Monitor* was taking waves over the pilot-house. It was clear they were moving directly into a storm system of considerable magnitude. By afternoon the wind had freshened again, to gale force, and the sea grew increasingly turbulent. A small amount of water started to enter the ship, but nothing that the bilge pumps could not easily handle.

The *Monitor*, which had no mast tall enough to carry the standard signal flags common to all ships of the navy, communicated with the *Rhode*

Island by writing chalk messages on a black-board and holding them up to view. As evening approached, Captain Bankhead scrawled a message informing the *Rhode Island* that if his ship needed help during the night, he would signal with a red light, which would be displayed on the same stubby mast as the ship's white running light.

At nightfall, the *Monitor* and *Rhode Island* were separated from the accompanying *State of Georgia* and *Passaic* by some five miles, and were running about seventeen miles southeast of Cape Hatteras, when they were suddenly hit by squalls. They soon found themselves "making very heavy weather, riding one huge wave, plunging through the next, as if shooting straight for the bottom of the ocean," as the *Monitor*'s helmsman, Francis Butts, described it. The ship would rise on one wave and fall into the trough of the next "with such force that her hull would tremble, and with a shock that would sometimes take us off our feet." Everyone was acutely aware that the life-boats on board the *Monitor* had been removed to the *Rhode Island* for safekeeping.

Sheets of water surged out of nowhere and smashed against the turret, and as the turret "worked" with every pitch and roll of the vessel, it inevitably loosened the packing material at its base. The storm increased in fury, and when the *Monitor* rose on the swell, Butts described how "the flat under surface of the projecting armor would come down with great force, causing a considerable shock to the vessel and turret, thereby loosening still more of the packing around its base." The leaks grew larger and harder to control, and soon the water stood over a foot deep in the engine room, threatening to douse the fires and deprive the ship of all power. The pumps — even the one designed to handle three thousand gallons a minute — could no longer handle the inflow. With repeated violent surges, the upper deck began separating from the lower hull, and with every downward crash, more water was forced into the crevice that was opening up between the two parts of the ship.

A little after 10 P.M. the captain ordered the red signal lamp displayed from the top of the turret, and told the crew to prepare to abandon ship. In response to the signal, the *Rhode Island* stopped her engines to allow the hawsers to be cast off, at which point the *Monitor* forged ahead under the impetus of her own headway and came so close up under the steamer's stern that there was great danger that the two ships might collide, which would have sent both to the bottom.

The *Rhode Island* managed to steer clear and to lower her boats, and under great difficulties, the rescuers were able to make it to the stricken ironclad and to take off many of her crew. One of the lifeboats, after returning with a group of *Monitor* sailors, was preparing to go back for more when it was thrown up against the gunwales of the *Rhode Island* by the force of the towering waves and smashed into kindling. The other boat, now working alone, made a second successful trip. There were still four officers and twelve men in the foundering *Monitor*, and the exhausted rescuers, determined to reach them before the ship went down, started out once more, guided by the red and white signal lights still hanging from the pennant staff. As they looked into the darkness, the lights disappeared. They waited in vain for them to show up again, and knew then that the *Monitor* had gone down with all remaining hands.

From her launching to her sinking, the *Monitor* had lasted exactly eleven months, all within the calendar year 1862. In that brief but violent time span, she had saved the blockade, doomed the Confederacy's hopes of securing British and French recognition, and revolutionized naval warfare. Her influence in this last instance was both profound and instantaneous. Within two days of learning the news from Hampton Roads, the Royal Navy, the world's preeminent naval force, canceled the construction of all further wooden warships. The *Times* of London ran an editorial that must have warmed John Ericsson's anglophobic heart: "Whereas we had available for immediate purposes one hundred and forty-nine first-class war-ships, we have now two, those two being the *Warrior* and her sister *Ironside* [these were Britain's only ironclads]. There is not now a ship in the English navy apart from these two that it would not be madness to trust to an engagement with that little *Monitor*."

EPILOGUE: GHOSTS

In Boston Harbor, the grand old USS *Constitution* remains to this day a permanent celebration of American leadership in maritime innovation. When first launched in 1797, she was recognized as a radically new kind of frigate, and the ingenuity of her design contributed significantly to her outstanding record of battle.

In Groton, Connecticut, across from New London, the sleek USS *Nautilus*, now retired and open to the public, represents an entirely different aspect of American preeminence in nautical technology: the world's first nuclear submarine, the progenitor of the underwater fleet that was so largely responsible for the silent victory in that strange and terrifying stillborn global conflict we know as the Cold War.

Americans have always taken great pride in their maritime heritage, and there is little question that had the *Monitor* survived the storm off Hatteras, she would almost certainly have been preserved, along with the *Constitution* and the *Nautilus*, as a national treasure and a worthy focus of a nation's pride. It is not without significance that despite the absence of her physical presence, her memory continues to reverberate through the national consciousness.

One can feel it at the Naval Academy in Annapolis, where a large, battered sheet of the *Monitor*'s armor plate, clearly showing the marks of the *Virginia*'s shells, still evokes a powerful sense of her presence. Farther up the Atlantic coast, in New York, echoes of the *Monitor* remain scattered throughout the city that brought her into being: the heroic statue of John Ericsson in Battery Park, his left hand proudly displaying a model of his ironclad; a mile or so to the north, buried in the clutter of the commercial district, the street sign for Ericsson Place that marks where the Swedish inventor first showed Bushnell his "sub-aquatic system of naval warfare"; and across the river in Brooklyn, where the signs for Monitor Street still define the route to the long-extinct Continental Iron Works at Greenpoint.

But such tangible memorials of the ship are rare, and for the most part, her memory continues to be defined by those who were most closely identified with her creation and operation.

John Ericsson, certainly the central figure in her story, prospered as a result of her success. The Navy Department's subsequent orders for larger and more complicated monitors ensured his future security, and his financial independence made it possible for him to follow his interests wherever they might lead. In the postwar years he worked in a variety of fields, including steam, electricity, and solar power. Despite his increasing age, he refused to slow down. "I propose to continue my work so long as I can stand at a drawing board," he announced with typical determination and energy. Periodically, over his remaining years, he returned to his earliest interests, including the caloric engine, for which he always maintained a special fondness, and his old "hydrostatic javelins," or, as they were by that time called, submarine torpedoes.

He died of a kidney ailment at the age of eighty-five, on March 8, 1889, just one day short of the twenty-seventh anniversary of the Battle of Hampton Roads. He was buried in New York, but a year later his remains were returned to his native Sweden with full honors, carried home aboard the USS *Baltimore*.

One of Ericsson's mourners was Rear Admiral John Lorimer Worden. The *Monitor*'s first captain had regained his eyesight soon after the battle and within months had returned to active duty in command of the *Montauk*, one of the new, larger monitors. After the war he served as superintendent of the Naval Academy and commodore of the European Squadron. As a result of the wound sustained at Hampton Roads, his face, throughout the remainder of his life, retained an ashen pallor from the minute particles of gunpowder permanently embedded in his skin. He died in his home in Washington, at age eighty, in 1897.

Cornelius Bushnell, who prospered along with

Ericsson and the others in the *Monitor* partnership, went on to far greater wealth after the war, as one of the principal organizers of the Union Pacific Railroad Company, but subsequently managed to lose most of his fortune in unsuccessful investments in mining and other railroads. He died in New York in 1896, at the age of sixty-six.

Bushnell's good friend Gideon Welles continued in his cabinet post after the assassination of Lincoln and throughout the troubled administration of Andrew Johnson. In 1868 he returned to the Democratic Party, which he had abandoned before the war on the issue of slavery, and died ten years later at the age of seventy-six.

On the Confederate side, Stephen Mallory, who may be credited as the man who forced the construction of the *Monitor* by his insistence upon Southern ironclads, spent a year in federal prison following the war and then returned to Florida and settled in Pensacola, where he died in 1873.

The Battle of Hampton Roads was only the beginning of the war for the fiery Franklin Buchanan. He was again in command of a Confederate ironclad, in this case the *Tennessee*, when he was wounded for a second time, at the Battle of Mobile Bay in 1864. He survived another ten years and died at his ancestral home after having served as president of the Maryland Agricultural College after the war.

His executive officer, Catesby ap Rogers Jones, returned to Selma, Alabama, soon after the loss of the *Virginia*, to supervise one of the South's few iron works and to cast cannon for the Confederate navy. He died in Selma in 1877 in what has been described as an affair of honor.

While many of the principal players in the saga of the *Monitor* were able to leave the war behind them, not all were so fortunate. Lieutenant Samuel Dana Greene, who had played such an heroic and vital part in keeping the *Monitor* from foundering on her voyage south from New York, and who had served as her executive officer from her first trials to her final loss at sea, brooded for years after the war over the fact that he had not pursued the *Virginia* when he took over command after Worden was wounded. There were anguishing questions of bravery and personal honor involved, and despite Worden's public statements of support for Greene's decision to return to the *Minnesota*, the high-strung Greene, ravaged by guilt and self-doubt, continued to worry over the matter, growing increasingly difficult and paranoid as the years went by. Finally, on December 11, 1884, while stationed at the Portsmouth Naval Base, Greene, in what was reported as "a state of high nervous excitement," entered a ship house on the base, put a pistol to his head, and blew out his brains. His death is perhaps the only fatality directly attributable to the battle of March 9, 1862.

In 1973, marine archaeologists, using the navy's most advanced underwater search gear, were finally successful in locating the bulk of the *Monitor*, sixteen miles off the coast of Cape Hatteras. Apparently she had rolled over as she went under and her turret, doubtless because it had been jacked up so that its base might be sealed with oakum, separated from the hull and fell separately to the ocean floor, where it touched down moments before the hull, which landed on top of it. Today both lie half buried in the sand, overturned and intact, in some 220 feet of water.

In the years since her discovery, divers have managed to bring up a number of artifacts from the ship — crockery and glassware from the wardroom, a lantern, the ship's anchor — which are now on display at the Mariners Museum at Newport News. There are plans to bring up her propeller, the four-bladed, nine-foot-diameter screw specially designed by John Ericsson, and there is even talk of raising the entire ship, but that is probably beyond the reach of present technology, although not very far beyond it.

Should they ever raise the *Monitor*, it would, of course, be a magnificent achievement and could only add to her renown. But whether she is reclaimed or continues to lie forever beneath the roiled seas off Hatteras, her unique place in the annals of war remains unchallenged: To an extent never previously attained, nor ever likely to be equaled, she was precisely the right ship, at precisely the right place, at precisely the right time.

ACKNOWLEDGMENTS AND SOURCES

It is safe to say that this book never would have seen the light of day had it not been for George L. Gibson, publisher of Walker and Company. It was his initial enthusiasm for the subject that encouraged me to write it in the first place, and his thoughtful and discreet involvement throughout the creative process helped materially to shape and define the narrative. Evidence of his perceptive editorial judgment and boundless curiosity can be found on every page.

This retelling of the *Monitor*'s story is designed as popular history, so I felt free to use secondary sources and to benefit from the researches and hard work of previous writers. At the same time, the *Monitor* is probably the most thoroughly documented ship in American history, and anyone setting out to tell her story soon discovers that there is a rich supply of primary material ready to hand, which I incorporated wherever possible. It seems that everyone who had anything to do with the development, construction, operation, or demise of the *Monitor* was eager to tell the world about it, and their letters, reports, diaries, memoirs, articles, and other papers strain the facilities not only of the Mariners Museum in Newport News, where I began my search, but also the National Archives, the Library of Congress, the Naval Historical Center, all in Washington, and the U.S. Naval Academy at Annapolis. Nor will you go away empty-handed from the New-York Historical Society, among other institutions.

In preparing this account of the *Monitor*'s brief but spectacular career, I relied upon a wide variety of authorities, from whom I learned much, and to whom I owe even more.

PROLOGUE: HAMPTON ROADS, VIRGINIA

For its marvelous grasp of the broad view of the war, I relied on Shelby Foote's *The Civil War: A Narrative* (New York: Vintage Books, 1986), and for its equally broad view of the more specific naval war, I found Ivan Musicant's *Divided Waters: The Naval History of the Civil War* (New York: HarperCollins, 1995) highly informative. For a somewhat different view, I also found useful *By Sea and By River: The Naval History of the Civil War*, by Bern Anderson (New York: Knopf, 1962). Among works more specifically focused on the confrontation of the *Monitor* and *Virginia*, I owe a great deal to both *Duel Between the First Ironclads*, by William C. Davis (Garden City,

N.Y.: Doubleday, 1975), and *Thunder at Hampton Roads*, by A. A. Hoehling (New York: Da Capo Press reprint, 1993). As always, the Rand-McNally *Road Atlas of the United States* provided practical aid in helping me find my way to Newport News.

1. TOWARD A "SUB-AQUATIC SYSTEM OF NAVAL WARFARE"

For the early development of steam-powered warships, I am particularly indebted to *Steam, Steel, and Shellfire: The Steam Warship, 1815-1905*, edited by Robert Gardiner (Annapolis: Naval Institute Press, 1992), which, although it is curiously dismissive of the importance of Paixhans shell guns, provided a detailed account of how the navies of the world sought to adapt to the new means of maritime locomotion.

For material on Ericsson's life, I relied for the most part on *The Life of John Ericsson*, by William C. Church (New York, 1890). For the description of the USS *Princeton* and the incident of the explosion of the forecastle gun, I relied on the richly detailed and most interesting account in *The United States Navy: 200 Years*, by Edward L. Beach (New York: Henry Holt, 1986).

For details on Ericsson's 1854 floating battery, I consulted primarily *The "Monitor" and the Navy under Steam*, by F. M. Bennett (Boston

218

and New York: Houghton Mifflin, 1900), *Twenty-six Historic Ships*, by Frederic Stanhope Hill (New York, 1903), and *USS "Monitor": The Ship that Launched a Modern Navy*, by Edward M. Miller (Annapolis: Leeward Publications, 1978).

2. THE LOSS OF THE *MERRIMAC*

There are many excellent accounts of the confusion involved in the loss of the Norfolk Navy Yard. For my version I am particularly indebted to *Duel Between the First Ironclads*, as well as *Thunder at Hampton Roads*, and to the article "Disaster at Gosport," by Captain Kendall King, U.S. Navy, retired, which appeared in *Naval History* magazine, March-April 1996.

3. "IRON AGAINST WOOD"

One of the themes of this book is that the American navy played a more important part in the Civil War than many historians seem ready to admit. Perhaps one reason the Union navy's efforts have not received the treatment they deserve is that its story is so much less interesting than the story of the Confederate navy. The Southerners, with minimal resources, and armed only with vision, imagination, and daring, managed to mount a remarkably effective effort over four years, which devastated American merchant shipping for decades to come. All the federal navy did was to spend a lot of money and mount a huge blockade that eventually won the war. Although my subject has been the *Monitor*, it is impossible to tell her story without constant reference to Southern activities, and to cover that aspect I relied primarily on two excellent works, *Iron Afloat: The Story of the Confederate Armorclads*, by William N. Still, Jr. (Nashville: Vanderbilt University Press, 1971), and *The Confederate Navy: A Pictorial History*, by Philip Van Doren Stern (New York: Da Capo Press, 1992). An intriguing offshore account, *A History of the Confederate Navy*, by the Italian historian Raimondo Luraghi (Annapolis: Naval Institute Press, 1996), arrived too late to be a basic source but made for excellent reading.

For material on Stephen Mallory, I relied on *Stephen R. Mallory: Confederate Navy Chief*, by Joseph T. Durkin, S.J. (Chapel Hill: University of North Carolina Press, 1954).

I am also indebted to R. W. Daly's contrarian analysis in *How the "Merrimac" Won: The Strategic Story of the CSS "Virginia"* (New York: Crowell, 1957), which was stimulating and thought provoking on many aspects of the Battle of Hampton Roads.

4. ENTER MR. BUSHNELL

The story of how Cornelius Bushnell wheeled and dealed the *Monitor* past the Ironclad Board and into existence provides fascinating insights into the workings of the military-industrial complex as it existed in 1861. The man who knew the story best was Mr. Bushnell himself, who left at least three different accounts, all of which tell the same basic story, but with differing details, chronologies, and bits of dialogue. One of his accounts is in an 1877 letter to Gideon Welles, another is in the form of a series of answers to written questions submitted in 1885 by the editor of a New York publication called the *Mechanical Engineer*, and still another is in an address to the Army and Navy Club of Connecticut in 1894. All three of these accounts are included in a little book called *The Original United States Warship "Monitor,"* compiled by William S. Wells (New Haven: Cornelius S. Bushnell National Memorial Association, 1899). My account takes bits from all three versions, and if it includes any overlooked inconsistencies, I think it is only fair that Mr. Bushnell share some of the blame.

5. AN AERIAL INTERLUDE

The description of John La Mountain's balloon ascension is based on an article by Hunt Lewis in *The Day Book*, volume 2, issue 3 (March-April 1996), published by the Hampton Roads Naval Museum.

6. CONTRACTS, SUBCONTRACTS, AND AN UNWELCOME SURPRISE

For much of the material in this chapter, including the citing of the Honorable Erastus Corning as a sub rosa silent partner in the *Monitor* project, I am indebted to *"Monitor" Builders*, William N. Still, Jr.'s book on the companies responsible for construction of the *Monitor*, published in 1988 by the National Maritime Initiative, Division of History, National Parks Service, Department of the Interior, in Washington, D.C. The sweeping assertion in the second sentence of the chapter is taken virtually verbatim from Dr. Still's work. It was so good, I could see no way to paraphrase it without weakening it.

The text of the *Monitor* contract itself is from the previously mentioned *The Original United States Warship "Monitor."*

7. "ERICSSON'S FOLLY"

The details of the *Merrimac*'s conversion are derived in part from articles by John M. Brooke and John L. Porter, the two men principally responsible for her design, in *Battles and Leaders of the*

Civil War, the Facsimile Reprint Edition from the Century Edition of 1887–1888 (Harrisburg, Pa.: Archive Society, 1991).

The story of the construction of the *Monitor* is from various sources, but most important William N. Still, Jr.'s *"Monitor" Builders*.

8. THE RACE FOR HAMPTON ROADS

The material in this chapter, essentially a continuation of the previous one, is dependent on the same sources.

9. THE VOYAGE SOUTH

Primary sources include the account of Samuel Dana Greene, entitled "In the 'Monitor' Turret," in *Battles and Leaders of the Civil War*, as well as *The Letters of Acting Paymaster William Frederick Keeler* (Annapolis: Naval Institute Press, 1964).

10. THE *VIRGINIA* ATTACKS

There are a number of eyewitness accounts of the events of March 8, 1862, in Hampton Roads. For the most part, I relied on "The First Fight of Iron-Clads," by John Taylor Wood, and "Notes on the *Monitor-Merrimac* Fight," by Dinwiddie B. Phillips, both in *Battles and Leaders of the Civil*

War, as well as R. W. Daly's *How the "Merrimac" Won*, F. M. Bennett's *The "Monitor" and the Navy under Steam*, and *The Blockade and the Cruisers: The Navy in the Civil War*, volume 1, by James Russell Soley (New York, 1881).

The anecdote concerning Lincoln and the wedding of Franklin Buchanan's daughter is from *Lincoln and the Tools of War*, by Robert V. Bruce (Urbana: University of Illinois Press, 1989).

11. THE REACTION IN WASHINGTON

The story of Edwin Stanton's hysterical response to the news of the *Virginia*'s depredations of March 8, 1862, is well-known. The main source is Gideon Welles's diaries, as published in 1911, and while it is worth noting that Welles had reasons to make Stanton look ridiculous, his descriptions are supported by the notes of John M. Hay, President Lincoln's personal secretary, who was also present at the meetings that day.

12. THE BATTLE

For the battle itself, I relied on the traditional sources, specifically Samuel Dana Greene's account in *Battles and Leaders of the Civil War*, as well as Keeler's letters, the correspondence of Gustavus V. Fox, and others.

13. Aftermath

The equating of the significance of the Battle of Hampton Roads with that of Gettysburg is a reference to Henry Steele Commager, who made such an assertion at least twice to my knowledge, once in an introduction to *Tin Can on a Shingle*, by William Chapman White and Ruth White (New York: Dutton, 1957), and the other in an introduction to *John Ericsson and the Inventions of War* by Ann Brophy (Englewood Cliffs, N.J.: Silver Burdett Press, 1991).

The description of the scene in Jefferson Davis's office is from the account of the naval officer present, John Taylor Wood, in *Battles and Leaders of the Civil War*.

14. The End of the *Monitor*

My basic sources for the sinking of the *Monitor* are the account in *Harper's Pictorial History of the Civil War*, by Alfred H. Guernsey and Henry M. Alden, a Facsimile Reprint of the 1866 Edition (Avenel, N.J.: Gramercy Books, no date), and "The Loss of the *Monitor*," by Francis B. Butts, a survivor, in *Battles and Leaders of the Civil War*.

EPILOGUE: GHOSTS

For material on the discovery of the *Monitor*'s remains, and the recovery of certain materials from it, I am indebted to *Ironclad Legacy*, by Gary Gentile (Philadelphia: Gentile Productions, 1993). Gentile is an outspoken critic of the National Oceanic and Atmospheric Administration, the government body charged with overseeing activities concerning the *Monitor*, but his book is evenhanded and informative.

On a personal note, I would like to extend my particular appreciation to my neighbor, Victor Talliaferro Boatwright, whose insights into the subject of this book were always knowledgeable, and always useful; to Joseph Mosier, who provided me with the probable origins of the name Newport News (New Port Newce), a piece of esoterica that I tried mightily to fit into the text without success; to Moira and Cormac O'Malley who found the precisely right Irish prayer I wanted; my long-suffering brother Ormonde, who volunteered to slog through the whole first draft and saved me from several gaffes while vastly improving the syntax; and to my beloved wife, Belinda, who once again put up with me and all my tiresome foibles.